Temporary Sanity:

A Look Through A Teacher's Eyes

Temporary Sanity:

A Look Through A Teacher's Eyes

By **Fran Finn**

iUniverse, Inc.
New York   Bloomington

Temporary Sanity
A Look through a Teacher's Eyes

iUniverse books may be ordered through booksellers or by contacting:

iUniverse
1663 Liberty Drive
Bloomington, IN 47403
www.iuniverse.com
1-800-Authors (1-800-288-4677)

Because of the dynamic nature of the Internet, any Web addresses or links contained in this book may have changed since publication and may no longer be valid. The views expressed in this work are solely those of the author and do not necessarily reflect the views of the publisher, and the publisher hereby disclaims any responsibility for them.

ISBN: 978-1-4401-6160-5 (sc)
ISBN: 978-1-4401-6161-2 (ebook)

LCCN: 2009933021

Printed in the United States of America

iUniverse rev. date: 11/02/2009

Contents

Foreword

By Chuck Watterson

I graduated from college with a B.S. in education in the winter of 1994 and I was ready to conquer the world with what I thought to be the quintessential tools of pedagogy. When I first met Fran in the fall of 1995, I was amazed that the school would hire someone who did not run his classroom the way I was taught in my undergraduate education classes. That was the first day Fran started teaching me lessons about life.

Although the title of the book and the first chapter, "Anywhere But Here" might seem to foreshadow the ranting of a pessimist, it doesn't take long to recognize the complexities and style of a narration meant to be told in such a fashion. After all, when we speak of our lives and where we want to be, don't we often start off by relating what uncomfortable circumstances brought us to change in the first place? Perhaps it would help to read some of Fran's short stories about transition and self-awareness. They are a more succinct telling of the human condition told with blunt truth and extremely insightful discoveries.

Either way, you are in for an intriguing adventure of the life of an unconventional, yet brilliant man, who has been on a journey from a classroom in Downingtown, PA. to the most remote parts of the world and has collected many, many stories along the way. He'll tell you about his own dysfunction with his family and the good and bad of his teaching career. But in an adjacent chapter, in an almost poetic manner, Fran will zip you to one of the far reaches of the planet and like a traveling guru will relate his insights and epiphanies, like his delight at a woman in Caribou Crossing, who, despite the fact that she was only selling hotdogs, was extremely happy.

Sometimes funny, sometimes sad, and sometimes with a bit of history thrown in, this book will surely captivate its readers. Fran's recounting of some of these stories will make you love him, hate him, and even question his motives from time to time; but through it all, you will learn acceptance, pain, friendship, culture, loneliness, and the search for one's place in the world; all the lessons he taught me over the years.

Dedication
To my mother, Kate Finn.

Chapter 1
Anywhere But Here

"Mom, I don't want to go. I can't stand going there. Can I stay over Noel's house?"

"No, you're going so you, Ginny and Sheila get in the car. I packed the clothes you'll need for the week along with your church clothes."

"I can't stand this ride, move over Sheila. We always get stuck sleeping in the morgue."

I've had a dislike for Pennsylvania ever since the 1970s. My mother was raised there and I used to have to visit my grandmother. I hated visiting. My mother grew up in Hazleton. I thought it was kind of a rundown city. It always seemed dark and gloomy because it was a coal mining town. It didn't help that my grandfather, uncle and cousin were morticians. My other cousins lived in Chester which isn't the best environment. Chester is right outside Philadelphia and the area is known for crime and is somewhat dangerous, but that is coming from someone whom grew up in northwest Connecticut. My uncle and cousins whom lived in Chester were kind of cool, but my cousin Kevin walked on the insides of his shoes. When I was about ten, I asked Kevin, "Why do you walk that way? The outsides of your shoes look like they're brand new, and the insides are all worn out."

"Well, I've had five open-heart surgeries," he said.

"So how does that effect your feet?"

He shrugged. "I don't know, but that's what I was told."

"Here, I'll help you walk straight," as I grabbed his feet to fix them.

"Cut it out!" Kevin cried. "That hurts!"

That was a number of years ago and my "help" never worked with his feet. Later, Kevin went on to follow in his father's footsteps and became a mortician.

Visiting Hazleton was always difficult and strenuous for me. We kids were always told that we had chores to do. My grandmother lived above a morgue that her husband had owned. I never knew my grandfather because he'd passed away a long time ago. He had made millions, I was told, during the Great Depression. Supposedly, he received money from the government to build homes for the poor. He would then take that money, build a house, ask the government for more money to build a house, use the material from the old house, and keep the money. I guess in tough economic times people will do anything to survive.

We had to sleep on cots in the morgue, between the viewing room and the embalming room and it always smelled like formaldehyde.

"Mom," I would say, "I can't sleep here, I never can. Why can't we sleep upstairs? The guy in the embalming room stinks and the smell makes me sick."

My mother, who was brought to school in a hearse, said, "There isn't enough room and it's the live people you have to worry about, not the dead ones."

Although my sisters Sheila, Ginny and I always had to sleep in the morgue, our brothers Mike and Pat, were usually lucky because they were a few years older than us and didn't have to come to Hazleton with us.

One time Ginny and I were playing checkers, she couldn't have been more than fifteen years old and I was thirteen.

My uncle came into the room and said, "Ginny, I need your help."

"Okay, I'll be right there," she responded. "Fran, I have to go help move some bodies. Don't cheat while I'm gone."

"You have to help move dead bodies?" I asked. "Doesn't that bother you?"

She shook her head. "No, I've been doing it for years."

The caskets were in the basement, and my brother Pat once got in trouble for trying them out. All I remember about the basement is that the stairway was too narrow for the caskets to be brought down the stairs, so they had to be brought to the basement through another entrance somewhere. I didn't spend much time down there and never took the time to find the other entrance.

When my Uncle Tom found out that Pat was climbing in the caskets, he was irate. "No one will buy a casket if there is already hair in it!"

My aunt Karen lived with my grandmother for her entire life, and she would give us things to do once we got there. "You three—yes, you, Ginny, and Sheila—go out and prune the roses around the brick walls of our yard, and after that, I want you three to clean the apartment next door and then clean the three apartments behind the house."

"Aunt Karen, we don't really know how to prune roses. We have apple trees and grape vines at our house," Sheila said.

"Try, and you will learn."

"Can't you show us?" asked Sheila.

"You'll get the hang of it," Aunt Karen insisted.

I didn't know—and still don't know—anything about flowers, so I always hacked them to pieces. It had a lot to do with my not caring all that much.

"I'll be out in an hour to check," Aunt Karen told us. "Then you can start on this apartment." She pointed to the one next door. That apartment wasn't very big, so it was easy to clean, but the other one was three floors and took a while. It's hard for me to understand how the family had so much property and wealth but there was nothing left after my grandmother passed away. I was told that my grandmother squandered all the money that my grandfather had made. I don't know if that is true, but I tend to think it must have been. When my mother passed away from a diabetes-induced heart attack, my grandmother didn't attend her funeral. I was told that was because it was too far from Hazleton to Torrington, Connecticut, where the funeral took place. Still, she was her *daughter*. So when my grandmother died, I didn't go to her funeral. The major reason was that my grandmother hadn't gone to my mother's funeral, but also, I saw it as an opportunity to type my midterms for school. (I took off two days after telling school officials I was going to my grandmother's funeral).

One of my father's friends said, "Fran was the only one with the balls not to show."

Everyone else did. So, I was even happier that I refused to go when, years later, my father told me that my mother had been forced to leave home when she was four years old and had to live with her grandmother for a year.

"What could a four-year-old do to get kicked out of the house?" I asked.

"I'm not sure; she never came clean on that," replied my father.

We would visit my other uncle from time to time. He lived in Chester, and I liked the house because as a teenager I thought it was "cool" that they had MTV, which we didn't have at home. My uncle and his family had a great setup; the house was family-oriented and homey. Everyone was nice, and Bill was a good cousin. We even had Christmas Mass in their living room at midnight on Christmas Eve because my cousin's uncle was a bishop in Bolivia and he would perform the mass, I guess that was okay. I can't stand going to church, but that mass at my uncle's was almost fun. Ironically, when I grew up, I ended up teaching at an Episcopalian school. My father always said that I was working for the enemy because we are Roman Catholic.

Ginny and I used to kid about religion because we kind of thought it was a joke. Ginny asked my mother,

"Why do we have to go to confession if God is everywhere? Why do I have to tell this guy?"

"You have to be able to confess so that you can be forgiven," my mother would answer.

Ginny said, "Who tells the truth anyway? I always get the same thing: 'Say five *Our Fathers* and six *Hail Mary's*.'"

We used to get yelled at in church for talking. One time, the priest even came to our pew to yell at us. But religion was part of what we had to do. All my brothers and sisters went to Catholic school, until I got hit by a car while we were picking them up. I was running across the street to see them and since then I can't understand why people don't look both ways when they walk across the street. It was a hit-and-run, and the school closed soon after. I don't think it had anything to do with me. I don't know much about the incident, except that the car that hit me was a black Cadillac. I was in a coma for a while, was in a body cast for three months and had to learn how to walk again.

Twenty years later, I asked my father more questions about the accident after watching a documentary on the disabled.

He said, "When you woke up from the coma, your godmother was there, and she started screaming because your eyes started to flutter, and she thought you were dying. After you got out of the body cast, your brothers and sisters took turns helping you learn how to walk again around the dining room table. Your mother didn't want you to play contact sports because you had fractured your scull. I told her, 'Let him do what he wants.'"

So I played nine years of football and eight seasons of rugby. My father told me that I would have tremors for the rest of my life. Sometimes I feel like Gene Wilder in *Blazing Saddles* when he's in jail talking to the sheriff and says, "Yes, but this is my shooting hand," as his right hand shook.

One of my most embarrassing times was when I was in high school. Each of the officers of the National Honor Society had to give a speech at the end of the year; I was the treasurer. At the end of each officer's speech, he or she had to light a candle.

I was feeling confident until the secretary, Beth, who spoke before me, sat down and said, "I was so nervous." That rattled me. My parents said my speech was pretty good, but when I went to light the candle, my hand shook so much that I couldn't light it. I was so nervous that I inadvertently said into the microphone, "Shit," and then used my left hand to hold my weak right hand so I could light the candle. Everyone—about two hundred people—heard me and laughed. I laughed it off at the time, but since then, I'm a wreck when it comes to public speaking.

Because my right hand was so weak, I tried to learn how to write left-handed, but I wasn't very good at it. I used to have to rewrite tests in college and grad school because my right hand shook so much that they were unreadable. It was no big deal since I've been accident-prone my entire life and have learned to deal with it and even make fun of it. This year alone, I cracked three ribs and had to get seven stitches in the back of my head.

Anyway, the religion thing stuck. Even though I really don't like it, it's ingrained. I still say the *Our Father* and *Hail Mary* every night before bed—we always did that when I was a kid. My mother used to have all five of us kneel at the top of the stairs to pray before we went to bed.

Two of my aunts were nuns, and my grandmother used to say to my brothers and me, "I'll give you $1,000 to become a priest."

We'd all say, "Sorry, grandmother, that's not enough." We had to call her "Grandmother." No one could call her "Grandma" because she thought that was disrespectful.

My aunts who were nuns were very different from each other. Aunt Jane was my mother's older sister; I just avoided her. I don't think she liked kids. She died when I was about twenty-six and crossing the country on vacation. Every couple of days, I would call my father to let him know I was all right, and it was during one of those phone calls that he informed me that she had passed. I was in Utah—I was trying to hit every state in the United States before returning home, and because I was so far from Pennsylvania, I knew I wouldn't make it back in time for her funeral.

Aunt Cathy was—and still is—much nicer. She doesn't know that I resigned from my teaching job yet but she always sends me birthday cards. The thing I remember most about Aunt Cathy is staying at the convent with her. It was when I was about six years old, and I stayed there with Ginny and Sheila. We had to be real quiet. I got yelled at by one of the other nuns for playing with my remote-control car so she brought us down to the convent kitchen for ice cream to console us.

Other church mishaps continued. When I was in high school, my friends and I wanted to go to the beach in Newport, Rhode Island, one Sunday. My father said, "You can go, but you have to go to church first."

"No problem," I assured him. "I'll go early and change into my bathing suit in the car." I figured we'd leave at 5:30 a.m. or 6:00 a.m., and I could run into the church and grab an itinerary of that day's sermon, since I knew my father would quiz me on it. My father goes to church every day and goes early. He saw me sneak in and grab the itinerary and leave.

Later, when I returned from the beach, he said, "I saw you this morning in church. Guess what you're going to do now?"

"What? I was there?"

"Get in the car. You're going to church for two hours, and I'll be waiting out front so you can't sneak out. Have fun, and never do this again."

"You're kidding, right."

"No, get in the car, now."

Mason, a guy from my computer class, was there in his hockey uniform cleaning the church. His father was a deacon at the church, and Mason cleaned the church to earn extra money. "Fran, what are you doing here?"

"My father saw me skip church this morning and is making me sit here for a while, so I can think about my actions."

We both laughed.

Another episode with religion happened when I had to take piano lessons. We all had to take lessons because my father had taken lessons for sixteen years, and he thought our taking lessons would build character. It was kind of like when we all had to go to Broadway to see *Evita*. I hated it. Sheila was the only one who didn't have to take lessons—that was because she was an artist, but she had to take tennis lessons to make up for not taking piano. Sheila was the rebel. She did things and got away with things that I don't think any of the rest of us would have been able to do. She told me she would sneak out after curfew but never told me what she did. I guess, eventually, my mother found out and that was when my mother started waiting on the porch or sleeping in our beds until we came home.

I hated the piano. The teachers were mean, and I didn't learn much or do much while I was there. One teacher was about seventy years old and had me bring in logs for the fireplace for twenty minutes as she talked to her birds—and the lesson was only a half-hour. Another was an ex-nun who married an ex-priest. The sad thing was that the ex-priest was my computer teacher and I didn't do well in that class. The only thing that saved me was that Mason knew more than the teacher and would send us all the information.

"Mom and Dad, I can't stand this lady. She hits my hands with a ruler when I mess up. What is this? The 1930s?"

"Yeah, right, get ready for practice."

I said, "I am not going, I can't stand that lady," as I sat on the chair next to the front door. Then my mother smacked the hell out of me.

Not until twenty-five years later did I know why she did that, when Ginny said, "You don't remember?"

"I just said I didn't want to go."

"No, you didn't. You told her to fuck off."

"I did? I don't remember that at all."

"Well, you did."

"I guess I deserved it then."

"If one of my kids said that to me, they'd get more than just a slap. You lucked out."

A few years later, my father decided to take piano lessons again; the teacher came to our house to give him lessons. The first time he messed up, she hit his hand with a ruler, and he yelled, "Get the hell out of my house!"

When he told me about it, I had to laugh. My father is a doctor and went to one of the best medical schools in the country—and this woman hit his hand. I just said, "I told you years ago that she was doing that to me."

After graduating high school, I went to Providence College, a Dominican school, which I really enjoyed. (I enjoyed it too much, according to my father). Students were allowed to live on campus only for the first two years; then they were required to move off campus. Every hall in the men's dorms had a priest living on it. It really didn't bother me that much, but we had "parietals"—that meant that the girls had to be out of the dorm each night at a certain time, and the guys had to hand in their ID card to the security guard at the front desk of the girls' dorms. Students who didn't do this were fined twenty-five dollars. I knew a guy who pushed a girl out a second-floor window to avoid being given a fine, and she ended up breaking her leg. If a person was caught with a beer by the priest anywhere in the dorm it was twenty-five dollars per beer but that wasn't really enforced because a lot of the priests were half in the bag by mid-afternoon. They usually came back after classes, had a few drinks, and walked around the dorm at midnight.

Every dorm had its own chapel, which was cool when we had rugby masses, because they were fun, although the chapel wine was pretty bitter and tasted awful. That was when the father would bless the team each week for a safe and victorious match. Father Smith was our rugby proctor for the first couple of years that I played. He often showed up at rugby parties and bought me a bottle of tequila when I was elected captain my junior year.

"Here, Fran, let's share this."

"Thanks, Father, but my stomach can't take that stuff. I don't want to get sick."

"Fine, I'll take care of it," he said, as he started to do shots. Father Smith also was the priest on my hall during freshman year and would help us out the night before our Western Civilization tests. Western Civilization was a two-year requirement for everyone, and it consisted of history, English, philosophy, and religion. Father Smith was the religion teacher, and it didn't take long for everyone in the dorm to figure out that he was giving us answers to the religion part of the test. Father Smith wasn't happy, though, when our dorm registered the lowest grade point average on campus. He put a notice on each of our room doors about a dorm meeting one night at 6:00 p.m.. He also told the resident assistant to make sure we were all there.

When we were all assembled, he said, "You guys have the lowest combined GPA in the school. Do you want to know what it is?"

All of us said, "No."

"I'm telling you anyway. It's 1.25. Get your act together, or you will be out. Bill Cransk, I want to talk to you. The rest of you can leave. Get out of here, and do some studying. I'm serious; you will be kicked out and you won't get any money back."

I played football against Bill Cransk in high school. At Providence, he was always reading, but he never went to classes. He wasn't partying or anything, just reading. After he came out of his meeting with Father Smith, I asked, "So, what did he have to say?"

"I'm screwed. My GPA is .5. He asked if I had a brain because it was almost impossible to get a GPA that low. My father is going to kill me when I get home. As of right now—and I don't know how he did it—I have to move into a convent across town until my grades improve."

"Wow, I didn't think that was possible."

"Right, wow. I have to go and get my stuff. They're bringing a car around for me to go to the convent." From then on, I only saw Bill a few times.

The truth, at the time, was that all of us were just having too much fun to do much studying. We spent our afternoons shooting bottle rockets out the windows at kids going to class or throwing apples and oranges at the guard house. My brother Mike had given me a box of one hundred condoms about a week after I started school. I got lucky the first weekend of school with a girl I had met six years before in Cape Cod but that was the last time that year. So we ended up making water balloons out of the condoms and throwing them out the window.

After Father Smith moved on, we had Father James as the proctor of the rugby team. He would go to Cape Cod with us and hang out at my future roommate's summer home. Derrick was my roommate during my senior year and went on to get an accounting degree, but after graduation he became a fisherman and moved to Alaska. I never heard from him again after he moved, no one has. During Father James' reign, we made it to the

Division II finals and after finishing second, we went to the Division I finals. In the Division I finals we got killed by Dartmouth (they were ranked fourth in the country at the time) and then UMASS.

Tim Broth and I were the coaches of our rugby team. Father James was the proctor when we got suspended for excessive partying on the sidelines. At the time, we had to use public fields for our games and spent each morning before the match combing the field to get rid of broken glass, bottle caps, and rocks, but the police said we couldn't play on public fields anymore because of the excessive partying. It wasn't even the players; it was the spectators. I figured our 1989 season was over, but once, when I was hanging out at another friend's house, Tim showed up. He seemed a little jittery and flustered, like he usually did when he talked about rugby. He had played for years at Fairfield Academy. He was a lot more into it than me. I just did it because I was tired of football but I still liked to hit people. "I've got a plan Fran. We can play at Brown University, but we can't be called Providence College."

I went over to his house to talk about it. "Josh and Greg go get a keg and when you get back we'll figure out what 17 players will be playing." Josh was the president and Greg was the treasurer of the team. They were Tim's roommates. Josh played for the forwards and Greg played for the backs.

"Tim, we'll have to be discrete because we probably could be kicked out of school for this."

"Don't worry about it, Fran. No one will find out. Then we'll get them all over to talk about it. If we can't get hold of them at their dorm or house, you two check the weight room and local bars when you get back."

After two hours of drinking and playing some rugby in the back yard Tim said, "Okay, you guys, we have one shot at this, so don't tell anyone. We're playing at Brown, but we can't be called Providence College. Anyone have an idea for a name for the team?"

Jeff said, "What about EDC?"

I asked, "What's that mean?"

"Eat dirty clam."

"That works for me." Then we had sweatshirts made with the logo. We went on to place eighth in Division 1.

About fifteen years later I had another run in with religion when I asked a few students, "What do you want to be when you grow up?" I never heard this one before.

Johnson said, "A priest."

"A priest? Are you sure?"

"Yes, I've always had an affinity for the priesthood and would like to continue in that spirit."

"Johnson, you do know that you're at an all-boys school?"

"I don't care. *I want to be a priest!*"

"Okay, we get it." I thought it was odd that a ninth-grader at an all all-boys school would say that and he was kind of a jerk. The boys at this school were a little homophobic and at the time priests didn't have the best reputation. He had a twin brother who was just as bad, and they pretty much got the crap kicked out of them every day.

"Oh, one of my great uncles was Father McGivney, the founder of the Knights of Columbus, and there is a statue of him in New Haven, Connecticut. According to my mother, Father McGivney was to be canonized, but he hadn't performed two miracles within the one hundred years required to be a saint. The first miracle was the Knights of Columbus, but there wasn't another."

After a break from school Johnson came back and said, "My mother said he was probably Italian."

"Johnson, my name is Finn and his name was McGivney. My guess would be that he was Irish."

Chapter 2
Grad School and Get a Job

In 1991 my mother passed away from a diabetes-induced heart attack. She had been sick for years, and later on, I learned that the diabetes was the cause of her huge mood swings. The night before she passed, my mother, father, and I had gone out for dinner. My mother ordered swordfish but complained that it didn't taste right.

At the time, I didn't know she had diabetes, and I said, "Well, if you didn't eat so fast, it probably would've taste fine." I feel like a jerk when I think of it now, but I didn't know she was ill. The next day, I had just come back from lifting weights when I found out that she had passed. I was in grad school at the time, but after my mother passed away, I took up her duties and grad school took a backseat. I was trying to finish my thesis on "What the United States Press Thought of the French

Resistance during World War II." It was pretty boring, but I was almost finished with it. Back then, people did research by looking at microfiche, so I often got caught up in the sports section of newspapers of 1941, reading about football or college sports. The most I learned out of all my research on the French Resistance was that the press didn't say anything bad about President Roosevelt and that his wife, Eleanor, was good-looking when she was younger, which I thought was hard to believe.

After my mother passed away, I went back to see my advisor about completing my thesis—and learned that he had retired and moved to California. The secretary offered to give me his phone number.

"How's that going to help?" I asked. "I'm writing my thesis."

"I guess you'll have to find another advisor. You'll have to wait until the department head, Dr. Jackson, is done with class. It should be twenty minutes or so."

An hour later, he showed up. "Mr. Jackson, I need to talk to you about my thesis."

"It's *Dr.* Jackson."

"Sorry, but I've almost completed my thesis, and my advisor retired. What should I do?"

"What is it on?" After telling him, he said, "I'm sorry, but I don't approve of that topic. Your old advisor was a professor of French history and I'm a professor of German history. You'll have to choose a new topic."

"But I've been working on this for six months," I protested as he walked away and closed his office door.

I turned to the secretary, "What was that? Germany and France were in the war and the thesis doesn't even really have anything to do with that." She shrugged and

I left. Right away, I figured it was time to move on. I couldn't keep doing what I was doing, taking care of my father and trying to finish a thesis I didn't care about. Everyone was driving me nuts; I got pressure from my family to stay with my father because by that time, I was living there again, and from parents of students I coached. The parents said I was leaving my father in his time of need. The funny thing is that at that time I understood why my mother got so irritated when my father was late for dinner. I never got that until I had to cook meals for him. My father wasn't a low-end eater, and it was time-consuming to cook for him. When he was late, I always was irritated. I wouldn't say anything, because it was a tough time for everyone, but I'd be thinking, "Why didn't you call? I've been working on this for hours. Now it's all ruined." I felt like such a wimp because of my reaction. When we were growing up all of us came back home at different times because of the activities we were in and my mother always sat down with us as we ate. She could handle all of us and I couldn't handle one. And the food was always good, except for the one time I started eating undercooked shrimp, that was bad.

My father also threw out all of the recipes that I had gathered from my sisters and sisters-in-laws. He said he was just cleaning things out, and he didn't realize I needed the recipes, but I was upset—I had to cook things that I never had before, such as Cornish game hens and pot roast.

My dad and I have a lot in common. Neither of us likes to talk much, and when we do, it's really obvious that we don't want to do so. We also like our solitude. After my mother died and I was staying with my father, he finally said, "Screw what everyone thinks. You need to get out of here."

He knew that my graduate degree was going down the tubes, so we got a book that listed all the registered schools in America, and I picked out a few at random. I really didn't care where I was going; I just wanted to go away, almost as far as I could. Financially, I had nothing but I was willing to take pretty much any job.

In 1991 I applied to a bunch of schools and did receive a number of replies and inquiries. Most of them didn't turn out well, though. I did get an offer to teach Japanese history at a one-on-one school in Flushing, New York City, but I had only one semester of Japanese history in grad school and knew I wasn't qualified. I also had an interview at a public school in Albany, New York, where I was told that I didn't get the job, but that I had such a bad interview that the interviewer would ask me down again so I could practice. It didn't help that I wasn't certified to teach in a public school. He did say that he would call me to substitute, but I lived three hours away. The best bet I got was in Winchendon, Massachusetts. I went up to visit and was told that someone would call me in a month if I got the job. I didn't get that job either.

By this time, I had already told everyone that I was leaving—that was not a good idea. I did get a call from a school in Downingtown, Pennsylvania, and Dover, Delaware, asking me to come for an interview. At the time, Ginny had moved down to Chester which is about half-way between Downingtown and Dover and then married and moved to Media. I stayed at Ginny's house, and I can't imagine how they slept; it was right next to the train tracks, which caused the house to rattle every time the train went by. Ginny said that I'd get used to it. I was only there for two days; I didn't get used to it.

The first interview was at the school in Downingtown on a Friday. The assistant headmaster gave me directions on how to get there but told me the wrong exit, and I got lost. When I finally got there, there was only one other applicant. The assistant headmaster took me on a tour of the school, which took twenty minutes—and then I was offered the job. We looked over the 1600 acres of land that the school owned and all the buildings that the school had. It was on a farm and had silos, barns, cornfields, and bean fields—and it was in the middle of nowhere, which I kind of liked at first.

I had never been on an interview like that; I didn't even know if I was hired to be a history teacher. I was told that I was hired to be a house parent, but I didn't know what that meant because I'd attended public school.

"I really have to consult my father because my mother just passed away," I said. The real reason I didn't accept right away was that I had another interview on the following Monday in Dover.

The assistant headmaster was kind of abrupt. "I hope you aren't bullshitting me because I have to fill spots quickly. I want to know by next week, or we will hire someone else."

"Okay, I'll let you know as soon as possible," I said and walked out, kind of confused about the whole thing.

I hung out with Ginny and Mike over the weekend, and we discussed the job. The following Monday, I went to Dover to interview for the position of head football coach and to teach history. The interview with the priest was short.

"Sorry; you're too young and inexperienced."

I didn't really like the school much anyway, as it was in the center of the city, so I went across the street to the gas station and called the all-boys boarding school in Downingtown and told them I would take the job.

The first night I was there I was worried. I had a room that was smaller than my dorm room, and I had to share the bathroom. That first night there was a party for the house parents. The people at the party, I thought, were strange and seemed like misfits and that this was their last resort. All of the new house parents—there were about ten of us—sat around and drank some beers. There were about ten of us and we had a couple of cases.

Life as a house parent wasn't a glamorous job. I heard it was worse before I got there but it was pretty bad for me. During my time there, I had to do the kids' laundry, and I was given four hours to do it. Before I washed the clothes, however, I had to sort the students' clothes by their assigned number.

I made a deal with another guy, Bob, telling him, "I'll wash all the clothes if you sort them out." He agreed.

The washers were huge and old; they could fit at least a months load of dirty clothes for eighteen boys. Under the dryers I could see flames to heat the clothes. It didn't seem all that safe. I would bring all of the kids' stuff down at around 10:00 p.m., and then the next day I would get up and put them in the dryer. I eventually tired of doing the laundry like that, so I would stand there and push the button until the cycle was over.

Part of being a house parent was that we had to have something called "forced fun." Every Saturday and Sunday we had to make all of the middle school kids go down to the fields to play games. It didn't matter what kind of game but it had to last four hours. The cottages were also locked so the kids couldn't sneak off and go back to bed.

It was a weird time in my life. Things were strange and they got a little worse. Kids were doing things that I had never seen or even thought of. Sports were a requirement at the school, but kids would slice their hands with razors so they didn't have to go to practice; others would jump out second-floor windows for fun. One kid tried to smother another kid with a pillow and another started stabbing himself with a pencil. At one point, cleaning up after a kid who had urinated or defecated in his bed didn't seem like a big deal.

The only uplifting experience that year was a trip during spring break. John, an old high school friend that taught and lived in Connecticut, asked if I wanted to go to Labrador, Canada. When I asked why, he said, "Because I like the name. We can take my car and take turns driving. Can you drive a stick?"

"No."

"I'll teach you when you get up here. We'll go to the bowling alley parking lot. Leave as soon as the school day is done."

Once I got up there, at about 8:00 p.m., John gave some instruction, and we practiced for a while but I couldn't get the hang of it. I continued to grind the gears on his 1985 Rabbit until he finally said, "Forget it. You're wrecking my car. I'll drive."

The trip to Maine was painless, but crossing the border wasn't as easy. We looked ragged and were sent into the security office. We had to sit there for an hour, in front of what I presumed was a two-way mirror, and answer questions.

"Why do you have a Connecticut license and work in Pennsylvania?" I was asked.

"I know I was supposed to switch my license after sixty days but I've been busy."

"Get it fixed when you get back, or you'll be given a huge fine," said the security guard. And then she let us go.

When we got back to the car, everything in it was on the ground. The doors had been pried open. We figured that they thought we were smuggling in drugs. We put everything back, popped the doors together again, and got out of there.

"John."

"What?"

"According to your map there are no roads in Labrador. They have secondary roads but no real roads."

"That's okay. We'll go to Nova Scotia and hang out."

That was fine for a few days, but the water at the low-end places where we stayed tasted and smelled bad.

"Hey, Fran, we have some time to kill, so why don't we just go to Newfoundland?"

"That might be expensive, but I'll give it a shot."

The next day we bought tickets for ourselves and for the car to travel on the ferry. It took eight hours, as the ferry broke through the ice. It was fun for the first couple of hours because I've only seen ships braking through ice on TV. After that we had to find a place to sleep, as we couldn't afford a cabin on the ferry, so we slept in one of the hallways. A lot of people were doing it so it didn't seem like a big deal.

It was close to midnight when we got to St. John's, Newfoundland, and snowing pretty heavily, so finding a place to stay was a major priority. We knew that we could only afford one night and would be back on the ferry to return to Nova Scotia in the morning. We checked into the first hotel we could find. We didn't see anything while we were there. The next morning we left for the ferry. I went in to buy the tickets for us and the car, and then went back to see how things were progressing with going through customs.

"We're in trouble," John said. "The axle broke on the car as I was driving it through customs." Randomly, he called out to the crowd, "Does anyone want to buy a car?" And someone did.

I went back for the refund of the ticket for the car. When I got back, John had sold the car for four hundred dollars and was haggling about selling the cooler. He got another fifty dollars for the cooler, but there was still a bunch of stuff in the car. We had tools and tapes and just a strange combination of things that we carried onto the ferry.

The ferry ride back was about the same as on the way there. The only difference this time was that we were even shorter on money. Even though John had sold his car, it was Canadian currency, and at that time it wasn't worth a lot. I was also concerned about the questions we would be asked when we went through customs again. We had made such a scene on the way into Canada, there likely would be questions if we left the country without a car. I knew there was a charge for anything sold in another country, and we had no money.

Somehow, we subsidized our income by gambling on the ferry. I've never been a good gambler and neither has John, but on that eight-hour trip back we made three hundred dollars. That would pay the cost home and maybe more. Once in Nova Scotia, there was a blizzard again, and we had to walk from the ferry to the nearest hotel, which happened to be right up the hill. It wasn't very far, but it was damn cold. Once there, we called a taxi so we could get to the beer distributor and bought a case of beer. We figured we'd be there for a couple of days because of the storm.

Luckily, we only stayed one night and got on a Cessna flight to Boston. It was also snowing in Boston as we flew in and when we were about one hundred feet off the ground the plane started flying diagonally. I was looking straight at the ground and John, on the other side of the plane, was looking up at the sky. I thought we'd crash. When we landed, we had to go through customs again, and the one thing that got me through was my voter's registration card since they wouldn't accept my license as identification for some reason. I think they were just giving me a hard time. There was no other reason for it as far as I could see. The previous night I had told John that we had to get rid of the tools and tapes because that would only cause more problems with customs asking us questions about the car and he reluctantly agreed.

In Boston we had to find a cheap way to Hartford, another to Cheshire, and a taxi to John's house. It actually worked out fine, and the gambling money pretty much paid for everything. The next day I left for Downingtown.

I knew it was weird and very surreal, at least for me because I had been so conventional up to this point, but I really didn't have a choice. I had been comfortable in my own skin and was a little wary of what was going on. As a house parent life was mind-numbingly boring, but I had to make the best of it.

Another thing we had to check in at breakfast because previously, the school had a problem with house parents putting the kids to bed, then going into Philly to mess around and not returning in time for breakfast. We had to get dressed in a collared shirt and slacks to check in, but I never ate breakfast at school. Usually, I would go back to the cottage, change, and go somewhere else to eat. I never had an affinity for the school food. I always got heartburn and had to go to the bathroom within an hour—and when I was teaching, that was hard to do. I used to tell Joe Pattop, another history teacher that had been at the school for over forty years, that every year I had to train myself again on when I could go to the bathroom since we only had three minutes between classes.

One of the other house parents, whom had been in the military had lost his license so he couldn't do any of the trips with the kids that we were required to do. I'm not sure what he did to lose his license but I presume drunk driving because this guy could drink. Apparently, he had a lot of time on his hands because he rewired the middle-school so we could all watch Bishop Cottage TV where he lived. He didn't like a number of the other house parents and committed vandalism against them— he stabbed one person's tires and put soap in the gas tank of that house parent's car, and he deflated the tires on another house parent's car every night. I asked that house parent, Mike, why he didn't just stay up all night to find out who was letting the air out of his tires. Mike's response was: "If I do, it will only get worse."

I went over to the ex-military guy's cottage one night after we'd put the kids to bed. He always slept with the door open, and I thought it was so he could keep an eye on the kids. That wasn't the reason though, because he had bugged all of their rooms.

"Listen to this," he said, "That's room 210." After he listened to the kids' conversations, he would go to their rooms and give then a hard time. The kids never knew how he knew what they'd been talking about.

This person also had all the keys to the school, so he would steal food from the kitchen and cook it in the cottage. Then he climbed into one of the rooms of a kid he didn't like and beat him with a skate board. The kid, according to what I was told, was knocked out and never knew who did it. He never got caught doing any of this.

Jerry, the military guy, liked to play jokes on the kids sometimes, like when he tried to rig my cottage to make it seem haunted. One weekend when I was on duty alone, I let the kids sleep in the TV room. They got scared after watching a David Copperfield TV special, and one of them tried to levitate another. They said they wanted to sleep in my room—there were eighteen of them.

I said, "That's bull and you know it. Get out of here and go to bed."

The following weekend Bob, my co-house parent, was on duty so Jerry tried to make the cottage seem haunted with lasers and weird sounds. I don't think he completed the job, though, because Bob worked there for a number of years after that. After that Jerry left the school, I took over his cottage and spent my first few days pulling out the wires from the rooms he bugged. Accidently, I pulled out the phone lines, too. I never told anyone; I just blamed it on the other guy. I also found taped phone conversations of other faculty members. When I mentioned this to them some said that they knew and would say strange things intentionally.

During the first year of being a house parent, the assistant headmaster told us that we had to keep notes on each kid so that we could discuss any problems at the weekly meetings. I kept notes to the hilt because I was so damn bored. The assistant headmaster never checked our notes, so the next year I said screw it and didn't do it. That year, he checked, so I had to copy notes from Jeff, the other house parent.

That first year I had to share the bathroom with all the kids on the second floor. I didn't like sharing a bathroom with ten kids, so I would wait until they went to school before I took a shower. In that first year, I always had to go to the bathroom at 5:00 a.m., so I would wake up the kids at that time, banging on all the doors as I went down the hallway. House parents were required to wake them up, but the dean of the middle school said I was waking them up too early.

Mike Hock, the Dean of the Middle School, turned out to be a nice guy. He had been a Green Beret during the Vietnam War, so the kids were really scared of him. He taught eighth-grade history and made the kids stand at their desks if he thought they weren't paying attention. Then he would open up all of the windows, and it didn't matter what time of year it was. At the time there was also in-school suspension. He would give the kid a number, like 13,002, and tell the kid he had to keep subtracting three until he got to a specific number. The kid was on in-school suspension until he finished it. I saw kids paying others to help them finish. Then Mike would check it, and if it wasn't right, the kid had to do it again.

Some of the rules in the cottage were, at least I think, unreasonable. Kids had to be in their rooms by 9:30 p.m. and were not allowed to leave their rooms until the next morning. I found that hard to follow because sometimes at night, I had to go to the bathroom, but I had to tell the kids that they couldn't. We also had a strike system. If someone did something wrong three times, he had to either do extra chores or go to bed early. Back then, I used to have kids try to kick me in the testicles, or they would masturbate on someone's stuff that they didn't like. If I didn't follow the three-strike rule, I would get a call from Mike, who often roamed the cottages in the middle of the night.

Mike would call me and say, "Room 213's light is on, so do something about it." Mike must have stayed up all night because he called to tell me that all the time. Eventually, Mike and I figured out how to turn off the power in each kid's room. After that, anytime a kid was up too late, I would just turn his power off. That didn't help much in the morning but it got Mike off my back.

That first year I would substitute for various teachers, including music, about which I know nothing really credible (except that Pete Best got screwed). When I substituted for the assistant headmaster who was a history teacher, he told me to improvise. Improvise? Some of the kids were almost my age—I was twenty-three, and some of these kids in tenth-grade were twenty and big. It turned out that the assistant headmaster didn't really teach the class. He got newspapers for all of the students, and they just read the paper. They didn't have to do anything, so when I tried to teach a class, they'd get mad. If they had homework, they either said, "Get lost" or handed me some notes from another class. Even when I did grade their work, it was never included in their grade.

That first year I asked one of the teachers, who that had been there for over forty years, "How does this school survive?"

"I don't know," he answered. "I just show up for work every year."

From then on, I was a little apprehensive of the place. I was always skeptical and tried to keep a low profile because I wasn't sure what was going to happen to me at this place. The school never came clean on where all their money was going. I figured I'd suck it up for now and look for something else. I even applied to the FBI and the Secret Service, but those ideas didn't pan out. I guess I was too short—no, I'm sure there was more to it than that. Maybe part of the reason was that the FBI lost my application and then spelled my name wrong when they did reply.

I did apply to other schools to get out of my situation, but I knew that the schools replied on postcards, and I didn't want anyone to know what I was doing. I also didn't want to jeopardize any chance I had of getting a full-time teaching job at the school in Downingtown. I knew that Rich Davis, who lived on the third-floor of the main building and delivered the mail, looked through all the mail. He wasn't a civil servant, and I still think it was illegal. Rich used to steal my *Sports Illustrated* and then give it back after he was finished reading it. Rich also had a Doberman pinscher that roamed the halls all day and night. It was a nice dog, but if you didn't know the dog, it scared the hell out of you.

I used my father's address in Connecticut as an address for responses from the schools. He would then send them to me in a brown envelope. I guess the government thought I was doing something wrong because I was fined five hundred dollars for having two mailing addresses in different states.

Chapter 3
Job and Ireland

After that first year, things started to turn around. The assistant headmaster quit, so the tenth-grade history class was an open position. I was hoping things would work out for me by the end of the summer.

That summer I worked at a summer camp, teaching swimming and as a lifeguard, even though I wasn't licensed as a lifeguard anymore. A fellow house parent knew the woman who ran the camp, so that helped me get the job. The camp was in Philadelphia and difficult to get to. I didn't want to take the job, but my father said my brain would rot if I did nothing for three months. The majority of the kids were rich snobs, and I wasn't used to that any more. These kids were from rich families that thought the world owed them a living. I felt like an idiot doing it.

The last thing I did that was of any importance that summer was train for a lift-your-weight competition. I had lifted since I was twelve. Our junior high school science teacher, who was also our assistant football coach, got it approved that we could lift during gym class. That continued in high school because our football coach was our physical education teacher. I was in pretty good shape and continued lifting in college. Pushing the scrum sled helped a lot. In high school, I peaked out at 160 pounds during the football season and got down to close to 145 pounds during the swim season. I was never a big guy—at best, I was five-foot-seven and 160 pounds. I was the shortest center and middle linebacker in the league. In college, I got more serious, to the detriment of my studies, and got up to about 220 pounds. I would lift a few hours a day but really hurt myself when I was doing squats. I didn't have a spotter and was trying to squat 425 pounds. The first three times I did it were fine, but on the fourth time, I overextended. Usually, a person just rolls the weights off their back, but I had to roll it over my head. I felt like a loser, so I kept on lifting, even though it hurt.

After college I kept on lifting in Torrington and in graduate school. I got good at it and got up to benching ten sets of ten at 225 pounds. I kind of got big, and one guy wanted me to go into competition. When I moved down to Pennsylvania, I started to lose weight because I didn't like the food, and I couldn't afford to go out and eat that much. I started looking for a place to lift, but the place was pretty desolate. I couldn't find anything, a place to lift or a place to get Copenhagen. I finally found a tennis club, which had a small weight room. I joined a "Bench Your Weight" competition, but I wasn't ready for it. I was over the weight at which I wanted to compete, so I went to the gym the night before and did ninety minutes on the stair master to lose the two pounds I needed for the next day. I got down to 171 pounds—I lost the weight, but that's not a good move. I was dehydrated and sick all night. The next day, in an event I didn't think was a big deal, was a big deal. There were a lot of people. We were in teams of four; two guys and two girls. I was going out with Cathy at the time, so I thought we had a good shot at winning. Cathy was a trainer at the gym and in very good shape, to the point where she could flex her chest. It didn't work out that way, though. Since the place was so crowded, we had to warm up right behind the competition bench. There was one guy there—he used to play football for the Philadelphia Eagles, and he weighed 225 pounds. There was another runt there who weighed 130 pounds. I didn't feel well after a long night of not sleeping and shaking. I knew that a lot was counted when people were lifting. My brother lifted Olympic York Barbell competitions and said it was a difficult thing to do, and he was a really big guy. He wasn't much taller than me but he had to get custom made shirts made because his neck was twenty-two inches. When it was my turn, I didn't extend my arms enough. Mike, my brother, had told me that I would see a light go on when I hit my chest; red for stay and green for go. It wasn't that intricate, but there were four judges. As it turned out, I came in second, as did our team. I lifted 171 pounds thirty-one times but only twenty-five were counted because I didn't extend my arms. The little guy, at 130 pounds, won the whole thing. His team got a trophy, and our team got T-shirts.

The teaching thing worked out the following year, to some extent. I got two tenth-grade classes, but I still had to be a house parent. I didn't like it, but I would pretty much have done anything if I didn't have to live with the same eighteen kids. I needed to get my foot in the door. For the past ten years, the substitutes had been getting twenty dollars a class, so a full schedule was an extra hundred dollars a day, and that was a good deal. And I didn't have to do anything teaching as a substitute. I must have made an extra seven thousand dollars during my first year subbing. I also knew that every teacher made a different salary so when I went to figure out my bid price for the headmaster, I put a lot of time into it and figured I would ask for an extra $10,000 over the $14,000 or so I was getting paid as a house parent. My father was glad that I got the job because he figured I'd been a baby-sitter, even though he thought my bid price was too high. When the headmaster called me in, I didn't even get a chance to sit down and discuss pay. He just said, "I'll pay you three thousand dollars, and your two jobs are exclusive of each other."

"But you pay your substitutes twenty dollars a class," I protested.

"I do?"

Another house parent was waiting down the hall as I walked out, "So how did it go?"

"All right, I guess, but I didn't get what I wanted."

"I figured you wouldn't."

"He didn't even know how much he's paying his subs."

"You know, if they change the sub pay and people find out it's because of you, you're dead. How much are you getting paid?"

"Three thousand dollars, and I figured it out: that's $7.50 a class. I asked for more, and he said he would think about it and tell me at the end of the year. The meeting was less than five minutes."

The headmaster left a note in my mailbox after the final faculty meeting, saying he would give me five thousand dollars. It still stunk, but I took it anyway.

The time frame for the two jobs was bad, though. It meant that I only had a day off every six weeks because we were on a six-day rotation as house parents at the time. It didn't matter that much to me—it was 1992, and I was twenty-four. Today, I would have hated it. On my days off, I'd go camping along the Brandywine River with anyone who was available. They say the campground is the Philadelphia KOA Campground, but it's actually outside West Chester, which is about forty-five minutes away from Philly. When I went camping on whatever days I had off, I would get up at 5:00 a.m. so I could make it back to school in time to shower and get to my first class. The only time that went badly was when I fell into the Brandywine River when I was taking down my tent in the dark, and I lost my watch—and it had been a high school graduation present.

Camping along the Brandywine was a good time. I'd correct papers, cook outside, and drink a few beers. There were only a few times when it could have gotten ugly. The worst was when Jim and I had way too much to drink and started heating up coins, deciding we were going to brand ourselves. Luckily, we chickened out, but the next day we couldn't find the car keys. Apparently, Jim had thrown them in the fire the night before; at least, that's what we think happened. After a frantic half-hour, we found them. Everything but the keys was melted, but we were able to use them and make it back to school.

That first year, I ignored my brother's advice. He had taught for a year at a private school before going to law school. He told me not to do what he did, which was to prepare for the next day's class the night before, because it would take way too long. I had messed around all summer and didn't care enough to kill myself over preparing for class. I had gone to the Swarthmore College's library and prepared what I thought was an appropriate amount of information. I had taken notes on the information that I was told to teach—I would be teaching World Cultures II, and I needed to cover India, China, Africa, Europe, and Latin America. My time frame was from 1815 to the present. The textbook, however, didn't cover those years and areas. I tried to contact someone at the school to find out what to do but during the summer it's almost impossible to find anyone at a prep school who has useful information. I ended up kind of winging it.

I had been told by the academic administrator that I had to cover so many chapters and give a test every tenth day, so I did it. Since the textbook didn't have most the information I needed I spent time in the library gathering the information and informed the students where to get the information. My problem was that I had attended a public high school, so I figured that the school year was 180 days, as in public school, but it wasn't—it was about 160 days. The year before, having been a house parent,

I never thought about how many days there were in the school year; I just knew it wasn't a good time.

When I figured out the class material, I tried to plan it so that I covered a certain amount of information each day; I even dated the class days. It didn't work, though, because there was always something that came up. Half the students might be out of class for a sporting event or half the school was sick, and they had to open up the cottages during the day because the infirmary couldn't handle the number of kids. Many times, I thought that academics wasn't the primary focus of the school. The kids missed class for all kinds of reasons. Those kids in choir were out all the time. When I was in high school, being in the choir or in the theatre was the only reason needed for someone to get beat up. But at this school, even the toughest kids were in the choir. One of the students said that most of them only did it because they could travel to places on choir trips, like Europe and Africa. Once the school cut the budget of the choir, a bunch of kids quit, and the others refused to sing in chapel.

As it turned out, in that first year there were only about 132 full days of class. Teaching that first year was kind of hard since I didn't have enough time to cover the material. I also didn't even have a desk; all I had was a podium. I gripped that podium like I was on life support. I don't know how any of the kids learned anything because I talked so fast. At least some of them apparently learned something, though—one of my first-year students came back years later as the valedictorian of Ithaca, and he said my class did help him. He was going into the FBI. Another student, who later became a house parent, said that my class was like college because I didn't stop lecturing, I just kept going. He was from the Caribbean and at the time, he transferred out of my class because I was going too fast.

Still, I couldn't keep up with the schedule that I had set for myself. I had kids that were spitting on each other and fighting. It's a very different school now than it was in 1992. Back then, we had metal doors, so all the teachers just closed the door and did whatever they wanted. All of the doors had dents in them—we would sit there and watch chairs being thrown out of the windows, either next door or upstairs. Or we'd be interrupted by the teacher upstairs, who had the class above mine, when he cursed out the kids. It was fun for me, though—I never knew what was going to happen each day. Would there be a food fight in the cafeteria, or would I have to break up a fight in the hallway? Once, I had to break up a food fight in the assembly room while I was giving my final exam. None of these types of problems have occurred in the last ten years.

As for testing the kids, it was a crap shoot. I would have multiple-choice questions, true and false, fill-ins, and three essays. In the word bank for the test I would place fake answer, like teams I played against growing up, towns that I had been to, and bands like the Kinks or Bob Seger and the Silver Bullet Band. I figured that if the kids chose those answers, they really didn't know what we were talking about in class. I knew that from the start, because I would put the homework on the board every day, and a kid named John (who eventually went to Emory University) would change the homework assignment page. Then I'd get homework that answered questions about India when we were talking about

Germany. Which, quickly, made me realize that the kids weren't listening.

After that first year of teaching, I took the summer off. I wanted to travel, but the funds weren't there. I had done a bit of traveling prior to that summer. I went to Ireland in 1989 with my sister Ginny and Mike on their honeymoon, when I was in college. Mike's family went along, too.

Mike has family in Ireland, and we were going to stay at their houses. Mike's mother and father were from Ireland and their wedding gift was a cruise to America. His mother passed away before I was in the picture but his father taught at Swarthmore which made it possible for me to do research there. He also has since passed away.

Ireland was fun, and I wanted to stay, but after the first few days I'd had enough. At first I thought, *I'll graduate, go to Ireland, teach, and open up a pub.* I mentioned this to a woman I met one night. She responded, "Oh, that won't work. There are no jobs here, and no one would go to a pub owned by an American."

I took her on her word, and after about five days I didn't want to be there anymore. It rained all the time and after climbing Croagh Patrick, I was just tired of the place. Originally, Croagh Patrick sounded like a good idea. It's the 2,100-foot mountain where St. Patrick supposedly threw all of the snakes out of Ireland and created the 1,000 island that surround Ireland. Supposedly, St. Patrick's grave and a chapel were at the top of the mountain.

I later read that there were never any snakes in Ireland. Each year, however, climbing Croagh Patrick is a pilgrimage, and everyone said we should go; it wasn't fun. There is a path for most of the way, but for the last few hundred yards, we had to climb up rock. It took four hours to get up and then four hours to get down. It was above the tree line, and we were climbing with Mike's sister, who was a smoker. She cried when we got to the top because she couldn't breathe; she just sat on the steps of the chapel. Also, if anyone got hurt, someone had to go down to the base and get a stretcher to carry that person back down. There was a grave at the top of Croagh Patrick but that could have been anyone's—there was no way to prove it belonged to St. Patrick. Besides a carbon test to approximate the time-period. There couldn't have been any dental records or DNA testing. As part of the pilgrimage, people are supposed to walk around the chapel fifteen times while saying prayers. We didn't do that; we just tried to catch our breath and tried to make Mike's sister stop crying. Then we went back down. There was a pub at the base of the mountain but none of us drank because the climb had made us all feel as if we were going to throw up.

The following night was Saturday, and we went to a pub. We thought it was odd that the pub closed at 10:00 p.m. Mike asked a local, "Why is the pub closing so early?"

"Because we have church in the morning but tomorrow night the pubs are open until 2:00 a.m."

"Don't a lot of these kids have school on Monday?"

"Yes, but church is more important than school."

Mike left it at that, and his brother and I hung out with the town drunk; at least, that was what we were told he was. Before 10:00 p.m. we went to a real dive pub and hung out until it closed. On the way back from the bathroom, I showed Mike's brother Eric the toilet paper.

"Look at this stuff; it's wax paper. How can you wipe with wax paper? I have to save this and give it to someone at home. They won't believe it."

After the pub closed we planned to return to Eric's grandmother's house, but the town drunk—and he was really drunk—invited us to his house for a beer.

We didn't have anything to lose and since his grandmother's house was really cold and we had to share a bed, we decided to stay out as long as possible, but we were a little shocked by what we saw. This guy didn't have a house; he lived in someone else's burned-down house. We didn't need to use the front door because there was no side wall, so we just walked in. It had half a roof, and he had kind of furnished it with what looked like someone else's trash.

We sat down at the table, which had charred chairs, and he got us a couple beers. He slurred his speech and then started speaking in what we thought was Gaelic. After a few minutes, we both looked at each other and realized this was not a good situation. We didn't even say anything. We just got up and left. He didn't miss a beat; he just kept on talking.

Chapter 4
Next Year and Alaska

In 1993 I had to change my testing process because a kid and a parent said I was trying to trick the students. I really wasn't; I was just bored as hell, and I would call in kids from the cottage to give me ideas for fake answers. At the time, I couldn't afford a computer so I had to write the tests out by hand, and I wasn't the best typist. I had to give the tests to another house parent to type, but my handwriting isn't the easiest to read.

So I changed the tests to include only twenty choices in the word bank instead of the forty-six that had been in the word bank. Many of the students complained because previously the answers had been so obvious. There were fifteen fill in questions, and the twenty in the bank were close to the real answer; it actually made the test harder.

I wasn't fond of the academic administrator. I really didn't like any of the three that were at the school during my tenure. The first one thought I didn't communicate enough to the other teachers. He thought I was antisocial. One morning, I went in at about 5:00 a.m., and a student of mine named Mark was squatting outside the gym, which I thought was weird. Then he came up to my room. He was a smart kid but didn't get along with a lot of the kids because he was kind of eccentric. I asked him, "Why are you here right now? It's so early?"

"I thought we had a track meet," he said, "and I pride myself on being antisocial so I leave early."

I laughed because I felt the same way most of the time which got me into trouble with every administrator I encountered.

My first department head once said to me, "Fran, do you know why you were hired?"

"Not really."

"Because the academic administrator thinks the prep schools in New England are so good."

"But I didn't go to a prep school." My father thought that prep schools only babied the kids. I agreed with that because at prep schools—at least this one—students seemed to get an award for farting in the right direction.

"He doesn't know that you didn't go to prep school."

"But it's on my transcript."

"You've been here long enough to know that he doesn't look at that stuff," he said as he walked away.

The second academic administrator, as I was told by another teacher, didn't like me. He was the one who made me change my tests. I wasn't allowed to put notes about the day's lesson on the board, so I had to e-mail the kids the notes, which I thought was counterproductive. I also had to meet with him every other Tuesday morning for two years. It didn't take long for me to realize that I was under review. Most of the meetings were a farce because we talked about what new furniture I bought for my house or what I was going to do for my summer. But the first one was the day after I met with the headmaster. He had asked everyone to come up with three things about the school that needed to be improved and three things that were good about the school.

The major thing I said was, "Why do we have handicapped parking and braille on each door room number, but we have no handicapped access?"

"If any handicapped student comes to the school, he could live in Young or Jackson cottage, because they could get access through the back door."

I thought, *That is a bullshit answer because those doors have fire alarms on them, and he never said anything about the main building. There is no way a handicapped kid could get into the school, not to mention the tunnel the students have to take to get to school.*

The headmaster also didn't say anything about my teaching or having to meet with the academic administrator the next day. He seemed to be a little disinterested though.

The next day I met with the academic administrator, and he said, "The headmaster told me I had to fix you."

I didn't know what he was talking about. "I just met with him yesterday, and he didn't say anything."

"He doesn't deal with that kind of stuff," he said, handing me a packet of e-mail complaints about me from various parents—and it was kind of thick. "A parent is trying to get together a cartel to get rid of you, and I've listed their names. I also gave you the e-mails because I wanted you to read them. I would want to know if anyone was saying anything against me. The major complaint is that you are correcting their grammar and that your tests aren't flawless."

"I'm only following the Middle States guidelines for English across the curriculum. Man, I hate correcting their grammar, because it takes forever. So am I going to get fired?"

He said no, but I wasn't so sure.

I went down to my AP class, threw away the e-mails without reading them, and told the students to work on an essay. I didn't give a crap what those people had to say about me, and what was going to happen was going to happen. After that meeting, I set up times with the students to discuss why they lost points over grammar. I e-mailed all of my students, the library, the guidance department, and the academic administrator all of the details of when I would be available for discussion. I said I would be in between 4:00 a.m. and 4:30 a.m., during lunch, and during my free periods. I did that for about eight years before I said screw it. I was up that early anyway, but I got tired of kids not showing up, and I'd be sitting there for three hours before school started, which made for a long day. I thought, *I have to show up three hours before school and other people show up five minutes before school?*

The last couple of years, I didn't do it. I was tired of it; I never got anything out of it. Only a few kids used the opportunity, and my room became everyone's locker. After a while, I would open up the door to the main building and my room; then I'd go lift. It still made for a long day because we were required to coach a sport after school, even though I didn't coach anything I had played. I'd coached football, swimming, and rugby but now I had to coach track?

I threw for the track team in high school my first two years, but I stunk, so I didn't think I was qualified. My coach was Mr. Gooding. He was also my linebacker coach and swim coach. In football, he would put on a helmet and say, "Come and hit me."

We'd all be apprehensive until the first person went, and he knocked the hell out of him with a forearm to the head. In swimming, he was just as tough. One time, he hit a kid in the back who was on the starting block—he used the long wooden pole that was used to save drowners, and it broke over the kid's back. He also taught me how to do backstroke flip-turns on the deck of the pool. Gooding would throw water on the deck from about ten feet away and then push my feet toward the wall, and I'd spin and push off. It hurt really bad, and I bled from my tailbone for years whenever I did sit-ups, but I can still do a backstroke flip-turn. Another thing he did was punish kids for stealing. It was easy to steal goggles or sweat clothes from other teams at state meets. All you had to do was walk over with your towel, drop it on whatever you wanted, and then pick it up. Two kids on my team were caught doing this. Gooding had the two kids bend over the starting blocks and the rest of us, all fifty, lined up with kick boards, and we were told to hit them as hard as we possibly could on the butt.

Brian, the captain of the swim team, was crying by the time it was my turn and said, "Fran, if you hit me hard, I will kick the crap out of you after practice."

I was in eighth-grade and didn't need the hassle. He also had something called opportunity. That was when you did anything wrong, drank to much water during football practice, or were caught, like I was, mooning kids in the stands at swim practice. Opportunity also had to do with getting to practice on time. The pool was at the YMCA, and it was about ten miles from the school. If you were lucky, you got a ride from someone else or you took the bus. School ended at 3:00 p.m., and practice was at 3:30 p.m. Opportunity consisted of running, pushups, and sit-ups for two hours. It wasn't fun. I tried it once when I was coaching football when this kid thought he was better than everyone else and wouldn't lift weights when I told him to. I made him run hills for a half-hour after practice. After the half-hour he threw his helmet at me and quit.

For track, Mr. Gooding used to have me throw the shot-put, discus, and javelin. I wasn't very good, but I guess that he thought that since Mike, my older brother, was all-state in the discus that I'd be good, too. I wasn't, but he would have me throw the javelin over and over again. When I did it, my hand would turn, and the javelin would hit me in the back of the head and go horizontal. He'd laugh and ask me to do it again. I should have quit but my parents wouldn't let me.

The next year we had a new track coach, Mr. Adams. He was a nice guy and played football with my brothers before he got a track scholarship to Texas A&M for the hammer throw. He would have us try it, and it was really hard to do. None of us could throw it more than ten or fifteen feet, but when he would throw it, the hammer went about a hundred yards. He would invite the throwers over to his house for dinner the night before meets, so we could have a spaghetti dinner for the carbohydrates. My parents let me quit track after Mr. Adams was killed in a motorcycle accident. Apparently, he was waving to a friend, lost control of his bike, and ran into a telephone pole. Supposedly his chest was ripped open by one of the metal spikes that comes out of the telephone pole.

I've seen this before, because I have been to a lot of funerals, and the mortician tries to make the person look like he normally would. I know that they have to sew the gums shut and sometimes have to tie down the limbs so that they stay in place. I learned about rigor mortis from watching Bugs Bunny cartoons when I was a kid. When I went to the funeral, Mr. Adams was in the usual clothes he wore, including his leather jacket.

When I went up to the casket, his mother said, "The team just had dinner with us a few days ago."

Anyway, I had to coach track. It wasn't that bad—unless it was a Saturday meet. They were about ten hours long and we usually had to go to another state because our school was too small to compete with any local schools.

One time, when we had to go to Delaware, a student named Kevin said, "I didn't know Delaware was a state." That's the kind of mentality many of the students had. They just knew what was right around them and nothing else.

I coached track for three years, and we won the league title twice by simply outnumbering the other teams. Most of the kids went out for track because the head coach only had an hour practice, while the other sport, soccer, practiced for two or three hours.

When I first started coaching track, the athletic director asked me and another new coach to go to a track conference at the Milton Hershey School in Hershey, Pennsylvania. I didn't want to go and told the athletic director it would be useless for me to go, because all the field conferences were on Sunday— and I had to be back early on Sunday because I was on duty. The athletic director wanted me to go anyway, so I hung out for the weekend, and the other coach went to the long-distance conferences, since he was going to coach them. The other coach had never played a sport in his life, so he wasn't psyched about it. It turned out that when we got back that the other coach was coaching the long-jumpers. He didn't know anything about the event.

At the end of the 1994 school year, I drove up to Woodbury, Connecticut to see John and then on to Torrington to spend the night with my father. He had moved from Cheshire to save some money on rent. He and I were hanging out that night drinking a few beers, and he said, "Why don't we drive to Alaska?"

I wasn't sure that was a good idea. John had just bought a new truck and wanted to try it out, but I didn't have much money and was cautious on how I spent my money. Besides, I was supposed to go to Tim's wedding later that month. Tim and I had been captains of the rugby team in college, and I felt bad about missing his wedding—but I chose to go with John. I called Tim and said I couldn't make the wedding because of some car problems. I doubt he believed it; we haven't spoken much since.

The next morning I packed a bag: one pair of underwear, one pair of socks, and toilet paper—I never go anywhere without toilet paper; as far as I'm concerned, it's the secret to happiness. (If you ever run out of toilet paper, like I did in college, you'll know what I mean. We had to take showers after we went to the bathroom). Then I grabbed my sleeping bag and pad, and went over to John's and banged on his window. I always have my sleeping bag and pad with me because I never know where I'm going to sleep. "Lets go."

We did have a map but no game plan; we just got in the truck and went west. We figured we'd take turns driving each day and we'd do about eight hundred miles a day. As it turned out, the first hundred miles each day were the only ones that were the most difficult. After that I would just hang out and drive and John would do the same. At times it got boring. Each day we would get the paper and whoever wasn't driving would read the paper to the other person; even the comics. We'd describe the comics to each other so that the driver would understand. One day John, I guess, was really bored. He abruptly said to me, "Over the past eight hours, you have cracked your knuckles 1,878 times. It is driving me nuts."

After we finally stopped each day, we would find a place to camp, usually at a KOA if we could find one—they were always clean and safe. John had a two-man tent but two grown men in that tent was a little tight, and I was really getting sick of it. After setting up the tent, John and I would set up the tarp over our tent, in case of rain. After that, we would buy food supplies. For most of the trip, we lived off beef jerky, but at night we would buy real food. We started doing that the first day of the trip. John was a good cook, and we made cowboy stew the first night. I'd cut up whatever we bought that day with the only knife we had, and John combined all the other ingredients. We had plenty of spices to cover whatever food problems we might have and had a cooler to save the remains each night for the next day's meal. Each day we would add something to the dinner. The addition could be corn, peas, celery, or anything that was available or that we could afford. Every once in a while, we added some kind of meat—usually hamburger, but we tried to mix it up with buffalo or even elk (except that we were told that we had to kill the elk ourselves, which didn't work since we only had a knife). We always cooked over an open fire, and after dinner we would write in our journals; then go to bed. I always woke up earlier than John and would wake him when I got bored. If he didn't want to get up, I would collapse the tent. That really ticked him off, but he would get up, curse me out, and we'd get going. He wouldn't talk to me for a while—at least, not until he got a few sodas into him.

John had his way of getting back at me, though. One time when we were camping in Illinois, we happened to be in a dry town. That didn't work for us, so we drove over the county line to a bar. The place was dreary, with about fifteen people sitting on the stools around the bar. It was about 3:00 p.m., but they were already pretty drunk. When I came out of the bathroom, everyone cheered and clapped. I didn't know what was going on; then I found out they were cheering because John had told everybody that I would buy the next round. It cost me about forty dollars.

As we reached the Rocky Mountains, storms started to settle in. We had slept in that day, so it was going to be a semi-late night of driving. I was driving through the Rockies and finally said, "John, I can't see anything, and if we don't stop I'm going to crash."

"Okay, then pull over at the next rest area."

It was pouring rain, so we just sat there. Then we saw a light out in the distance, like a lantern coming toward us. We were in the middle of nowhere, and I started thinking about Ned Beatty in the movie *Deliverance*. I turned to John. "Fuck this," I said and took off. It stopped raining a couple of hours later.

By that time, it was too late to check into a KOA, but we found one and snuck in. We set up our tent and made sure we were awake and gone before the owners woke up the next morning so that we didn't have to pay. It was a crummy thing to do, but we didn't have many choices. We were also running out of money and had a long way to go. Both John and I had direct deposit and were paid by our schools every two weeks, but we didn't have a lot of savings and gas was expensive; it would only get worse in Canada.

From there we made it to Iowa. I think the people in Iowa are the strangest people I've ever met because they just kept to themselves and nodded at us as we walked by. They were nice but in an unconventional way. It just seemed weird.

We walked around town, and I kept saying, "Wow, I'm in Iowa," like I was mentally handicapped.

"Shut up, Fran, you're going to get us killed."

That night, we stayed outside of the city at a KOA, and we started to hear sirens. We weren't completely sure what was happening, but it was starting to get windy. We went to the front desk to ask what the problem was, and the owner told us that there was a tornado coming.

We both stared at each other: we were in a tent!

"What should we do if it hits?" I asked.

"Go down to the river and hang onto the base of a tree."

The tornado touched down, but it wasn't bad enough for us to have to hang on to any trees; we just hung onto the tent and ground so that we wouldn't be blown away.

After that, we had to go to Des Moines to get money. At that point, we had purchased a book that listed all the ATMs in North America, and the only place in Iowa that had an ATM was Des Moines. It was Sunday, and we didn't see any people—it was kind of eerie.

From there we headed north to Montana and then Michigan. We had no plan; we had months off and all the time to do what ever we wanted. In Bozeman, Montana, I finally got fed up with the tent. I couldn't stand it; I couldn't sleep that close to someone else, especially a guy, and by that time the tent was in bad shape. John had had the tent since he was nine years old and in the Boy Scouts, and it had seen better days, so I bought a four-man Eureka tent for two hundred dollars, and John did the same. From then on, I looked forward to sleeping.

Bozeman was a big city, but it had a small town feel to it. We hung out at a diner for a while, listening to the waitresses tell stories about bears walking down the middle of the street and that it had become so common that people didn't even worry about it any more. John and I hadn't seen any bears, but we would read anything that we could get our hands on about how to deal with them. There are plenty of different ways to deal with black bears and brown bears. One bear can't climb trees, but if attacked by the other, we were informed to play dead. We weren't taking any chances. Each time we set up camp, we urinated around our camp site in about a thirty-foot radius to keep the bears away. We also made a lot of noise and stored our food in the truck. Eventually, especially as we got farther north into British Columbia, the Yukon Territory and Alaska, we would strip off our clothes before bed and throw them as far away from our tents as possible. We had read that people would go to bed after cooking but not change their clothes, and the bears would pick up the scent and tear through the tents, looking for food, and killing the people.

I peeled a piece of bark off of a tree and placed a sticker on the back as a surface on which to write a postcard to my brother. I wasn't sure it would work, but I wanted to try. I wrote to Mike: "Moving to Montana soon; going to grow me a crop of dental floss." I thought he'd get a kick out of the Frank Zappa reference, and he did actually get the card.

By that time, I wasn't worried about attracting bears if I was naked. I hadn't bathed in three weeks and was pretty grimy; I hadn't brushed my teeth or anything. My clothes were falling apart. My jeans were worn out, and my underwear was past the point of it's effectiveness. I had on a sweatshirt from Martha's Vineyard that my sister Sheila had given me, and my shirt had holes all over it. My Timberlands had cost a lot, and now the soles were falling off. (Since then, I've bought boots from K-Mart that have lasted longer). Obviously, I wasn't the person to get a room the night after a rainfall. A number of times our tents were too wet, and it was raining. We had to stay indoors and dry out the tents, so we would hang them around the room. John got tired of having to get the room whenever our stuff was wet. I'd try, but because I hadn't bathed or shaved (and my beard doesn't come in evenly), I looked like a psycho. I had chew in my teeth, and I'm sure I smelled pretty bad. Most of the time I was told that there were no vacancies. Then John would go in, and we'd get a room. John hadn't showered either, but he never got as greasy or slimy as I did. Somehow, his hair always looked all right, and he was kind of clean. I looked like I'd woken up in a gutter, but I didn't care; I was having fun.

Recently, on our last trip to the Dominican Republic, John told me that one of the reasons that he asks me to go along with him is that people in these areas don't normally see people who look like me—short, stocky, and somewhat imposing. (That's not the kind of look I was going for, but I'll go with it).

After Montana, we headed to Michigan to cross the border. We were about ten miles from the border and camped at another KOA. This KOA was building new cabins. The KOA cabins are really nice; I have stayed in them all over North America. We lucked out this time—there was leftover wood after building the new cabins that was being given away as firewood. We filled up the back of John's truck with wood and headed across the border.

The border agent asked, "Is this wood for building or firewood?"

We had prepped for this and replied, "For building." Since we knew that Canada treats their wood differently, and the chemicals used in Canada aren't the same as in America.

We were let in, and we had enough wood for at least a week.

In Canada, we went west on Route 1 toward British Columbia. The scenery was great and the wildlife was even better. We finally saw our first bear, and I happened to be in the passenger seat at the time. We stopped as it was crossing the road, and I rolled down the window to take a picture. The bear was about ten feet away. We both did this a number of times—until we read that a couple had been doing the same thing. They rolled down the window, took the picture, and as the reel of film was rewinding, the husband looked at his wife—and the bear bit the back of his head. We knew then that we were done taking pictures of bears with the window open.

We reached Banff that day, and along the way we saw a wolf. We weren't really sure what kind of wolf it was, but it was just hanging out there on the side of the road. We both thought it would make for a good picture. John got out of the truck and got about five feet away from the wolf to take its picture. The picture came out great, and later, I had it blown up and would bring it to class to show the kids.

As we drove away, an ambulance was going to pick the wolf up since, I guess, it was injured. When we got to the resort town of Banff, we looked at postcards with photos of wolves and found out that the wolf we'd seen was a timber wolf, that they travelled in packs, and that they were very dangerous. We just looked at each other, as if to say, "Whoops!"

From British Columbia, we headed north to the Yukon Territory. I loved the Yukon Territory because there was no one there. It's about the size of California, but there were only about 32,000 people that lived there when we visited, and 27,000 of those lived in the capital city of Whitehorse. They had no doctors and only a few nurses in the entire territory. We stopped at a number of places to camp; a few are memorable. The first was Watson Lake. This was purportedly the second largest city in the territory, with two thousand people. It was very remote, and we even visited the Sign Post Forest— the place where soldiers from World War II put up signs from their hometowns.

During the war, the United States knew it needed a fortified road to protect Alaska from the Russians even though they were an ally—Siberia isn't very far across the Bering Strait from Alaska. Supposedly, when U.S. soldiers were building the Alaskan Highway, they felt homesick, so they put up signs from their hometowns, creating the Sign Post Forest. We took off the front license plate from John's truck and posted it there.

Watson Lake was fun at first. We got to the campground, and there was a bin of wood, so we just filled up the back of John's truck with as much as we could and settled down for the night. We hung out and cooked dinner, drinking beers. We could tell there were a couple guys through the woods. We couldn't see them, but they were singing Neil Young songs at the top of their lungs and seemed to be very drunk. Neither of us cared until we heard, "Welcome to the Great White North," and they started shooting a rifle—we didn't know if they were shooting into the air or in our direction.

It didn't matter where they were shooting. It scared the hell out of both of us. We collapsed our tents, threw them in the back of the truck, and left. I hung on to the tents out the back window. We ended up driving about four hours north and slept on the side of the road.

We stayed at another place in the Yukon Territory, although we didn't stay long. After putting up our tents, we were getting ready for dinner. Then a kid and his dad came out of the woods, right by our campsite. The dad spoke to John, saying that he was living off the land but would appreciate some food. I was watching the kid, and he started eating leaves off of the tree right next to me.

"Don't you think your son will get sick if he eats the leaves?" I asked.

"No, he does that all the time."

The guy kept pressuring John for food and beer and said he was going back to his home and would be back. The kid followed him, so we grabbed our stuff and left.

The next place of interest was Caribou Crossing; fifty people lived there. We stopped at the welcome center, and John got out to find out where we could camp. I just sat in the truck, looking at the fat lady selling hotdogs at her hotdog stand. I was amused by her exuberance in selling hotdogs in such a small town. She really seemed to enjoy it, and I was glad for her. When John got back, I pointed her out, but he didn't seem to care.

We found a place to camp but after a while, we got bored and decided to go into town for a few beers. Standing outside the bar, we caught the scent of marijuana that seemed to be coming from around the back of the bar, but we went in anyway, and there was no one there.

We had a couple of beers, and then John went up to the bartender and asked, "Where are all the people?"

"They're at the rec center. Every year at this time, there is a town party."

So we decided to join the party. At the rec center, we bought tickets for beer and at first, it was a great time. There were people there from Michigan who seemed to be having way too much fun. Then I saw the hotdog lady. Somehow, we locked eyes, and she started walking toward me.

"John, shit, I think she's going to ask me to dance," I whispered. "I hate dancing."

"Don't worry about it; just have a good time."

The woman grabbed my arm and said, "You're dancing with me."

John just laughed. Then she turned to him and said, "You're next."

After she finally let me go, John said, "Let's go," and we walked out.

The next place we stopped was Whitehorse. Compared to the rest of the territory, this place was excellent. It looked like any major town in the United States, except that everything was really expensive. I bought a couple of shirts, but I still hadn't bathed yet. I was hanging onto that and started to take pride in the thought that I hadn't. It had been so long that I wanted to see how long I could hold out. How long could I handle it, and how long could people around me handle it? Now, I was on a quest to be as dirty as I could be.

From there we continued north. We had been told at the beginning of the Alaskan Highway that it was paved the entire way up, but it wasn't. The glaciers wiped out the road each winter, so movement was slow. Some of the trucks they used to fix the roads were so big that John's truck could drive under them. He was a little worried because his truck was new.

We were still in the Yukon Territory, and it was the last stop before the Alaskan border. We had about two hundred miles before we hit Alaska but felt confident we would make it—until we met an older couple from Rhode Island who said, "You do know that you need four hundred dollars each to get back into Canada."

"What? Why?" I replied.

"Because Canada doesn't want transients."

I looked at John. "I only have fifty dollars in the bank."

"I only have twenty dollars, so I guess we'll have to wait ten days until our direct deposits clear."

"Well, we'll find something to do. Thanks for the information," I said to the couple. Then we headed off to have some of our cowboy stew.

Once we entered Alaska, we headed north to Fairbanks. On the way we saw a sign that read "Exit Glacier," so we did. I had never seen a glacier up close and thought it would be cool. There was a sign that read, "Do not stand on the glacier. It is dangerous!" Both of us said screw that, and we climbed on to the glacier. John propped up his camera on one of the posts with a sign that instructed us not to do what we were doing, and we took a picture. After that, a couple did the same and asked John to take their picture. For some reason, he decided to be a jerk and cut their heads out of the picture.

"Why did you do that?" I asked.

"I thought it was funny, and they won't even know until they get the film developed."

We stayed there for the night and planned on going up the Dalton Highway the next day to the Arctic Circle. We needed a few things first. We had read up on the Dalton Highway and knew that it was right next to the Alaskan Pipeline and that we needed to bring extra gas, an extra fan belt, and other essentials. We needed all this because gas stations were sixty miles apart, and the dirt road wasn't in the best of shape.

We grabbed all that we could afford to buy and left that morning. At first the road wasn't that bad; then, as we continued, we gathered that the trucks had the right-of-way because they would fly by us at 60–70 mph, and we were going maybe 20 mph. As the trucks passed us, they kicked up all kinds of gravel that bounced off John's truck. John started to panic, and he got even worse when a rock hit and cracked the front windshield.

After a while, we started following two guys in a beat-up car, riding on their tire rims. We followed them into the gas station and knew that they were going to pay a lot to replace their tires. We filled up the truck and started to leave when we realized that we had a flat tire. Luckily, we probably popped it on the way into the gas station. It didn't cost much to repair. If it had happened anywhere else, it would have been dangerous to repair because of the trucks flying by and the debris that they kicked up.

We continued on up the Dalton Highway to the Arctic Circle and decided to camp there. We did the customary thing of taking our picture in front of the Arctic Circle sign; then we set up camp after closing off the area we were in with branches, so we wouldn't be bothered by other people. The camping area was all dirt and because of the permafrost, the trees were very small. Then I collected rocks for everyone in my family, so they could have them as paperweights from the Arctic Circle. (It turned out none of them believed me when I said where I'd collected the rocks. Shit, I carried those rocks close to six thousand miles, and they just threw them out. It kind of ticked me off). I also found a piece of petrified wood while we were making a fire. I carried that home also. John dug up a small tree and carried that home. Both of our actions were illegal because people aren't supposed to carry minerals across country borders, but we didn't care.

We cooked dinner and did our ritual of urinating around the campsite and throwing our clothes as far away from our tents as possible. It didn't get too cold; about 35 degrees in the middle of the night. I'm sure the summer solstice had something to do with it since the sun never really went down. That was a little hard to get used to. The animals never knew when to sleep, and I didn't have a watch so many times I woke up thinking it was morning—and it was midnight. I'd walk around and then collapse John's tent. I did that the morning after his birthday. I had gone to bed early that night which made him angry and he walked to a bar. I have no idea when he got back but he wasn't in a good mood.

The next morning we continued north on the Dalton Highway, trying to reach Prudhoe Bay that day. We made it as far as Coldfoot. Coldfoot was a village of fifteen people, and across the road from Coldfoot was Hotfoot. We found out that Hotfoot was where the prostitutes stayed while men were building the Alaska Pipeline. We decided to take a look until a man came out of his trailer with a shotgun, which caused us to head back across the road to Coldfoot.

Next, we stopped at the convenience store, hoping to grab something to eat, but it wasn't a convenience store like Wawa or 7-Eleven; it had tires, fan belts, and oil. It was about 8:30 a.m., and we asked when everything opened and how much it would cost to stay in the hotel. The "hotel" was actually a number of trailer homes hooked together. I didn't really want to stay there, but I did want to see what the rooms looked like. It didn't help that they cost over $140 a night.

"Nothing opens until 5:00 p.m.," we were told, "and there is no beer."

"How far to Prudhoe Bay, then?"

"About sixty miles, but there's no reason to go there because they just got three feet of snow, and the town is dry because it is where the Alaska Pipeline begins."

So we went back down towards Fairbanks and stopped in another town named Livengood. Only seven people lived there, but we didn't see anyone. All the houses were made out of pieces of tin, and there was trash everywhere—old fridges, washers, and dryers. I thought that was odd because it looked like they didn't have electricity or running water. We stopped to look for food, but that was a bust.

I was driving down the Dalton Highway when we started to get pummeled with rocks again. The front windshield was broken six more times.

"Pull over!" John said. "If my truck is going to get messed up, at least I want to be the one driving it."

Then we came to a part of the road that they had started to tar. Up there, they didn't use a steam roller to level out the tar; they just let the cars do it. Tar was getting all over the truck—on the sides of the truck and especially under the truck. All of this caused John to get more ticked off. When we finally reached Fairbanks, we asked a local what to do about the tar on the truck. He said we had to de-tar it with kerosene, so we bought a shit load of kerosene and spent the rest of the day getting the tar off the truck.

Later, we found a campground outside Fairbanks and checked the engine—it had been making strange sounds. Once we opened up the hood, we saw the problem. A muskrat had eaten into the radiator. It probably climbed in to keep warm. It was plenty warm by that point because we had been driving all day and had cooked the hell out of it. We had to get that fixed the next day.

After that, we headed toward Valdez. At Valdez we ran into the guy who ran the campground.

I asked, "What's the difference between a province and a territory?"

"You tell me," he responded. "You're the history teacher."

I thought, *Shit, it's Canada. Who cares? I was just being nice.*

According to this guy, the difference was that a province elected its own representatives, and a territory had theirs appointed by the government.

From there we headed to Seward, which had great scenery, even though I'm not much into esthetics. We camped right by the ocean and watched bald eagles most of the day. We still had a few days before we got paid, so we decided to hang out there for a couple of days until we could afford to leave. That day, John and I got into a fight about his driving. He liked to drive with no shoes on, and I thought it wasn't safe. From there it, the fight, escalated to complaints about my cracking my knuckles and complaining about how much Copenhagen tobacco cost. It was obvious that we were really getting on each other's nerves, and it bothered me that John was a control freak.

"I'm going to get wood," John announced as he climbed into the truck and took off.

After about two hours, I thought, *That jerk left me here; he's gone.*

After a couple more hours, he came back with wood and had cooled off.

"I thought you left, asshole," I said.

Laughing, he said, "It took me forever to find wood."

The rest of the afternoon, we watched people run up and down the mountain about a hundred yards from the campsite. Some had their dogs with them. "John, what the hell do you think those people are doing?" I asked. "I've been watching those people all day."

"I'm not sure, let's ask the park ranger and maybe give it a try tomorrow since we can't afford to do anything anyway."

She said, "You guys can try, and you don't have to worry about the bears once you're above the tree line."

John and I stared at each other, both of us with a "what the fuck?" look on our faces.

That night, a woman asked John if he could help her get her camping stove started. Then she gave him a huge slab of halibut. We found some butter and tin foil, and we broke off three twigs—two with V's in them and a third straight one. We set that up over the fire after wrapping the tin foil around the stick. We turned it a number of times until we figured the fish was cooked. It was the best dinner we had on the trip.

Later on, a strange guy with blond hair came to our campsite and asked, "Can I have some of your chew?"

"No, it's too expensive," I said.

He opened his mouth. "You guys want to see where I got shot through the mouth and all the teeth I lost?" Then he said, "Lets go down to the high school and pick up some girls."

We both said, "No, that's all right, and here's some chew so you can leave now."

The next day we headed toward the mountain. There was no single trail; it just divided and went in all kinds of directions. It also was at about a 45-degree angle. After about a half-hour, I was hanging on to a tree limb and yelled, "John, I don't think I can do this!" But he wasn't there when I turned around.

"Okay, let's get down," I heard him say. He must have been twenty yards to my left.

After that we went to the welcome center and found a booklet on the mountain. It was called Mount Marathon, and there was a race there each year. We learned that at least five people die there every year. Most of the people die because on the way down, they just run as fast as they can, and they run into trees. The winner of the previous year ran the whole mountain in less than fourteen minutes.

What a moronic idea that was! We went back to the campsite, and because we had nothing to do, I decided to take my first shower. It had been close to a month, and I was looking pretty bad. Before taking showers, we went out and bought new clothes. I bought everything new: underwear, jeans, shirt, socks, and boots. The soles of my boots were almost all the way off, and there was no way to save my underwear. Since we had no money in the bank, we had to charge it, which I didn't really want to do, but my choices were limited. When we got back to the campsite, I stripped down and burned all my clothes; including the boots. I knew burning the boots was wrong because of the rubber, but I didn't care.

The shower cost two dollars for seven minutes, so I had to rush to get as much scum off of me as possible. I finally didn't smell any more but I still looked scary because the water ran out before I could shave or brush my teeth.

That day, we met a teacher from a bush town who was traveling around Alaska during his summer break. We asked, "How many kids do you have in class?"

"About ten, ranging from kindergarten to seniors in high school, and I teach all subjects."

"Do the kids enjoy school?"

"No, but it's the only warm place in the winter. Each kid is required to bring at least one log for the fireplace, and the kid who brings the most logs gets to sit the closest to the fireplace."

The next day we headed toward the border and went to the last bank with an ATM that we could find. The problem was that we couldn't take out more than two hundred dollars each. We said screw it and tried anyway. We knew that it would take at least a week of serious driving if we were to make it back to school on time. When we got to the border, I expected some trouble, not just because we didn't have enough money but because we both looked a little ragged, even with our new clothes. I always have a problem at borders; it doesn't matter how much I try to look professional. The border guards always seem to think I have something to hide. This time, though, we weren't questioned.

We made it back to Watson Lake that night and started to pile on the wood again—and then we read a sign that indicated it was up to two years in prison for stealing wood. We looked at each other, and I said, "That sign wasn't there on the way up." So we put back all of the wood and took only what we needed. This time our stay was better. No one shot at us.

The next day we were hoping to reach Washington. When we finally got to Washington, John went out to buy food. While he was out, I shaved, but when John saw that I'd shaved, it ticked him off. "We agreed not to shave until we got back home!"

"Yeah, but I'm scaring people."

"So what?"

"That's easy for you to say; people don't cross the street when they see you coming."

After that, we headed down to Oyster Bay, Washington. It's reported to be the oyster capital of the world. I don't like oysters, but I figured I'd give them a try while I was there. We went to a dive bar and ordered up a couple of beers.

"Why is this beer red?" I asked.

The bartender said, "Around here, we drink a beer with tomato juice in it."

We tried it, and at first it was good. I haven't had it since that day, though, and would never recommend it, because the after-effects weren't as pleasing. It ended up giving me heartburn.

I said to John, "I think I'm going to try the mountain oysters."

"Do you know what those are?"

"I saw Chevy Chase eat them in a movie once, and I know they are bull balls."

"You're going to get sick, and we're in the middle of nowhere."

Instead, we both ordered stuffed oysters. After that, John got up to go to the bathroom, and this squirrelly looking guy sat down next to me. He was dirtier than I was and was covered in tattoos.

He said to the bartender, "I hate fucking tourists. I just want to cut their fucking throats."

I thought, *Great, at least I'm twice the size of this little mother, and I'm pretty sure I can beat the hell out of him.*

John got back just as our oysters arrived. I ate them and didn't think they were that bad. I wouldn't order them again, but at least I didn't vomit.

When we got to the parking lot, however, John bent over and started puking.

I said, "Huh, and you thought *I'd* get sick. Give me the keys. I'll drive."

We continued having a few beers at the campsite and John fell asleep on the picnic table as I wrote in my journal. John kept mumbling, "Mmm, Jenny. Mmm, Jenny."

I knew who Jenny was; John had dated her years ago.

At that point, the owner of the campground came over and saw John; then he gave me a bucket to put all our trash in and possibly for John to throw up in.

The next day we headed towards Oregon, where we blew out a tire again. We stopped at a gas station, and it took two hours for the attendant to pry through all the tar under the truck, where the spare tire was stored. He didn't complain at all, though.

From there we headed east and ended up east of Salt Lake City. As we were driving up a huge hill toward Park City the transmission dropped and we could barely move. We found a campground and headed out for supplies.

We couldn't believe how many beautiful women we saw.

I said, "What the hell is this? Everyone here is perfect? What the hell is Park City?"

We didn't know it was a resort town. While we were leaving the shopping center, I noticed this Inuit woman collecting carts. One of the carts got away from her, and I started to go over to help her out, but she looked right at me and said, "What the fuck are you looking at?"

I thought, *Damn, lady, I just wanted to help*, and I left.

Dropping the transmission caused us to lose a day, but at least it happened outside of Salt Lake City, which had the largest Ford plant west of the Mississippi River; John's truck was still under warranty. We planned to go to the plant the next day.

That night, we bought some beer and then walked up the hill behind our tents to watch the stars for a while, which sounds wimpy but we didn't have enough money to do anything else. John tried to take a picture of Venus, which was bright in the sky that night. Suddenly, I saw something that caused me to tug at his shoulder.

"Leave me alone," he said. "I'm trying to get this picture."

I kept tugging and pointed at the ground next to his leg—there was a porcupine standing right next to him. Those things hurt. We just watched it walk by like we weren't even there. Then I got a long stick and tied some string to the end. We had been watching these fish swim down the stream all day and thought it would be fun to catch and cook one, but we didn't have any bait. John bent a paper clip for the hook, and I cut off some of his hair for a lure. We tried corn, peas, and even gum, but none of it worked—but it did keep us occupied.

The next day we drove back to Salt Lake City and got the truck fixed; it took about four hours. From there we continued southeast, ending up in Oklahoma, and camped on the edge of a cow pasture. We found some bones from dead cows, and John kept a jaw. After that, we decided it was time to get back to Connecticut because school would be starting soon. I stayed at John's that night and was off to Downingtown at 4:00 a.m. the next morning.

Chapter 5
Middle States and Yellowknife

What threw me off in 1994 was that we had a new academic administrator that year, and he didn't know anything about history. It was also a Middle States year—that meant that a committee was sent to our school that would monitor our classes and see if we met required state regulations. Damn! That meant I had to be good. I was used to talking the way I wanted and acting like I wanted. If a kid deserved a smack, I gave it to him. If another kid was unruly and someone smacked him to shut up, I'd say, "You deserved that." Most of the teachers were like that back then. With the committee coming, I'd have to pretend I was someone I wasn't.

The academic administrator also thought it would be a novel idea to teach American history backwards; he thought that would impress the Middle States committee.

I had never heard anything so stupid. History cannot be taught backwards. It doesn't make sense—there's no cause and effect; there's effect and cause. Eighth graders can't figure that out; they didn't care in the first place and weren't willing to try to put together this puzzle. After a while the kids got frustrated.

"When is this Henry Clay guy going to die?" someone asked.

I said, "Sorry, guys, he's only getting younger." It was a pain but the academic administrator was hell-bent on it. As it turned out, the Middle States committee never even entered my room, so teaching that way was a waste—the eighth-grade kids learned nothing.

In my classes, I would use the school as an example of the feudal system. We had the hereditary king—the headmaster, whose grandfather founded the school; the nobles (the administration), the peasants (the students), and the serfs (the teachers). I thought it was a great way to relate feudalism to the kids. The headmaster was born into the job, the administrators were given special privileges, the students were treated poorly, and the teachers were treated even worse and were tied to the land. If they lost their job; they lost their house. It was a perfect example, but I started to get into trouble for using it. Eventually, I got an award from the advisor of the student council as a gossiper. I was only trying to relate history in a way the kids could understand, but the school administrators didn't see it that way.

The school built itself up to be like a utopia, but that form of society never works. I discussed utopian societies with my classes. We discussed Sir Thomas More, Adam Smith, and Charles Fourier, who actually waited at his house during lunch, every day for twelve years, for someone to give him money to start a utopian society, but no one came. We even discussed Robert Owen's setting up New Harmony in Indiana, where people would live and work together for the common good of society. (It failed after five years because everyone started driving each other crazy).

People had been telling me to watch out about being to outspoken since I started working at the school. I tried, but I really didn't like not being able to be myself.

An administrator once sent me an e-mail, telling me that my e-mails weren't "fluffy enough." What the hell did that mean? He said that I should read the e-mails sent by the guidance department to get an idea of how to send an e-mail. Theirs usually began in the same way: "Good morning. I hope all is going well," or "Good afternoon. I hope your dog is doing well."

I mentioned this to my class and asked, "If I e-mailed something like that to your parents, what do you think they would say?"

Most kids just laughed and said, "Our parents know you're not like that."

"You're right. I hate to say it, but I don't really care how your parents are doing. My job is to tell them how their son is doing."

By that time it was getting close to Spring Break, and I wanted to set up a trip with John. I said I wanted to go as far north as possible and decided on Yellowknife, Northwest Territory. He said he would think about it, but in the end, he decided not to go. I wasn't sure I wanted to go alone, but the next week I had a ticket to Yellowknife.

As Spring Break got closer, I started to warm up to the idea. *Screw it*, I thought, *I'll go by myself.*

I started to get psyched. Before I left on my trip, I drove up to Torrington to visit my father, and on the way back I bought three bags of mulch to weigh down the back of my truck. The next day I had packed a small bag of clothes. I had called ahead to the information center to find out the weather, and they said it was about -50 degrees during the day and got colder at night. They also gave me some advice on what kind of clothes to bring. I had bought some fleece, long johns, and warm socks. I had reserved a room at the Northern Lights Hotel. I didn't bring a hat because I thought I looked stupid in a hat—turns out that no one cares what you look like when it's -50.

I headed off to the Philadelphia airport and a flight for Edmonton, parking my truck in long-term parking. I planned on being away for ten days—that would get me back at least a day before school started again. The flight to Edmonton was uneventful. When I got there, I had a two-hour layover. The first thing that happened was that I was pulled out of line by security. They asked for my passport, and I told them I didn't have it with me—at the time, a passport wasn't required to go to Canada. Then they sent me to the security office, and I had to talk to a supervisor for a half–hour, explaining why I was going where I was going. Finally, the officer laughed since I guess, he was just busty my chops and let me go. I went to the bar and started talking about my background to an older guy I met. He told me about his business and then gave me his card; he said that if I was ever in Edmonton again, I could stay with him. I thought, *That is not going to happen.*

There was an announcement that directed passengers where to go to board the flight to Yellowknife—it was in a remote part of the airport. When I got there, there were only fifteen other people—I was starting to think it was a big mistake.

I asked the attendant, "Is there any way I could come back early if things don't work out?"

He shook his head. "No, we only fly in and out of Yellowknife every ten days, and it's a national airport." I learned later what he meant by that comment because the airport was really small.

I knew I was kind of in an unfortunate situation since I had already paid and wasn't happy about what might happen, but I figured I would try to make the best out of it. When we got on the 747—all fifteen of us—we spread out throughout the plane. I guess I looked a little nervous because the flight attendants kept coming by and giving me food.

We landed in Yellowknife in a blizzard at about 10:00 p.m. The airport was about twenty miles outside of town and was about to close because of the storm, so I knew I had to find a cab real soon. I wasn't sure of the actual temperature, but I was colder than I've ever been. A fellow passenger must have figured I was uncomfortable with the situation and told me that he would get a cab for us. He said that I shouldn't stay outside for more than ten minutes at a time, or I would get frostbite.

In the cab, the driver pointed out local spots, saying things like, "This is where you can pick up prostitutes," or "This is where the strip joint is."

"I don't plan on doing either of those," I assured him, "but how can a prostitute stand outside in this weather?"

"They don't; you have to go inside the building."

"Thanks, but I just need to get to my hotel."

When we reached the Northern Lights Hotel, I paid the $100 a night that it would cost for the next ten days. The desk clerk, who had a wooden hand, led me to my room. I tried to go to sleep but soon turned on the TV. I couldn't get to sleep because someone seemed to be flushing the toilets, one after another, every twenty minutes.

The next day, I asked the cleaning lady, "What's with the toilets flushing all the time?"

"They flush to keep the pipes from freezing; you'll get used to it."

I called my father so he'd know where I was. When I told him the name of the town, he said, "Jesus Christ, where the hell is that?" He quickly looked it up and said, "Get back here as soon as possible."

"Sorry, I'm stuck here for the next ten days."

The maintenance people felt free to enter the guests' rooms whenever they felt like it. It didn't matter if I was sleeping or in the bathroom; they just walked in and said, "Sorry, just replacing the fridge," or "Just fixing the TV."

On the first day, I decided to find the information center. I wanted to gather some material for class. I also listened to the advice of the man at the airport and stopped in certain places every ten or so minutes to get out of the cold—the air was so cold, it hurt my lungs. I asked a few people for directions, but no one seemed to know how to find the information center. Finally, I met a nurse, who said, "It's about two miles outside of town, but be very careful if you decide to go—there are no roads outside of town."

"Yes, I guess people travel by snowmobile."

"That's right," she agreed, "but you'll be walking, and two miles in three feet of snow can be difficult."

"Thanks, I'll follow the snowmobile tracks so it should be a little easier." On the way out of town I noticed that there were jumper cables coming out of all the houses, and there weren't many people walking around.

I stopped at a tavern to warm up, but it seemed overly warm. "Damn," I said, "why is it so hot in here?"

A person sitting next to me said, "Because it's so cold outside and a lot of times people need to warm up quickly to avoid frost bite when it's so cold outside."

"Isn't that the opposite of what you are supposed to do? Shouldn't a person be warmed in increments so that the body isn't shocked?"

"What the hell are you talking about?"

"Oh, forget it," I said, and I moved across the bar. I started talking to a woman there because I wasn't sure what was going on since so many people were dressed up. "I don't mean to pry, but what is going on here?"

"My father-in-law died, and we're having the funeral here."

"Sorry, but why here?"

"You aren't even close to being from around here are you?"

"No."

"The ground is frozen, so we can't bury him until the spring."

"It is spring."

"Not here."

I got more uncomfortable and decided to leave. As I walked out of the tavern, people were bringing in the body. I then traveled down the snow-stricken road to the outside of town. The snow was a couple feet deep and seeped into my boots and socks. Following the trail was a good idea at first but because of the snow drifts, the tracks were hard to find.

Once I reached the information center and started asking a few questions, the attendant said, "Oh, you must be the American. I took your call. Do you know what fleece is now?" as she laughed.

"Yes, thanks, and could I have as much information on the territory as possible?"

"Sure, here you go."

The information she provided was interesting but there wasn't a lot of material that I could use. I did learn that Yellowknife was the only city in the Northwest Territory that had roads, but by that time, I already knew that. It did explain, though, why no one turned off their cars—that way, they wouldn't have to jump-start their cars, and there was no danger of anyone stealing the cars—where would anyone go? The other thing I learned was that Yellowknife had 17,000 people, and that if you spread out everyone who lived in the Northwest Territory, they would be twenty-three miles apart.

Then I made the trek back to the hotel, again stopping a number of times hoping to warm up my feet. Damn, the ground was like ice cubes; my boots just stuck to it. After a couple of days of walking so stiff, I hurt my back and had to spend a couple days taking baths to reduce the knot in my back. One day as I was doing that someone knocked on my door. It was a really drunk Inuit woman, who stood about four-foot-two. She walked into my room and said in a slur, "I don't live here."

"I know you don't," I answered. And she turned around and walked out.

The following day I asked a lady that worked at the hotel, "Why would someone just come to my door and walk in?"

"If someone calls and asks for 'the American,'" she replied, "we just send them to you."

I drew out a breath. "I'm not sure that is the best way to handle it."

She shrugged. "That's our policy. You don't know enough about the people up here. You just happened to come to town when the Inuits are coming in for their two-week break after spending six weeks mining for gold. They travel in clans and sleep together while mining. I'm pretty sure you can put the rest together."

"I was kind of wondering why I saw so many mentally retarded people and midgets."

She said, "It's a little bit of that, but they come into town and drink the entire time, wasting their money. Usually, they are pretty out of it."

The next day I went to the bar next door and struck up a conversation with an old guy. He had just finished reading his paper and offered it to me. "Here, you can have it. This place is so small that I know you're not from around here. The paper only comes out every other week."

"Thanks, I'll hang onto it for one of my friends who teaches journalism. Could you tell me what people do for a living up here?"

"Sure. I'm a bush pilot. I used to transport dead bodies, but because the bodies would release gas when I hit a certain altitude, I couldn't stand it any more. Most people are trappers, fishermen, or miners. They also usually have more than one job because the cost of living is so high."

"I did see a program on TV on my first night here that showed how much money a person could expect to pay on utilities that month. This month was $900. Geez, I don't spend that in a year."

After that, I met a couple who had moved to Yellowknife from Edmonton. They said they drove up, and it took them a month because none of the roads were paved. They were working as bartenders at one of the local bars, and the man asked me to stop by that night. When I did, they were watching *Road House* with Patrick Swayzie. He asked, "Are all American bars like the one in this movie?"

"None that I've been to," I answered, "and I've been to some hairy places."

"How long are you going to be here?"

I said, "Just until tomorrow. I have classes on Monday."

"That stinks because next weekend we're having a town party. Everyone goes, and it's great. If you don't buy one of these pins the police put you in jail for the weekend. It's all a joke, and it's for charity, although I don't know which one."

"Maybe it's for your heating bills, I can't be here, but I'll buy one anyway. I can afford the two dollars."

Later that night, an overweight Inuit woman came up to me, "Are you going to the town festival next weekend? I see you have your pin."

"No, I can't. I have school on Monday and just bought the pin for the hell of it."

"Where do you go to school?"

"I don't go to school; I teach at a small school outside of Philadelphia, Pennsylvania."

"Where's that?"

"In the United States."

"If you stay for the week, I'll put you up and pay for your ticket back."

I thought that the people here were either the nicest people I'd ever met or something was up. I thought she must be a prostitute. "Sorry," I said, walking away. "I have a nonrefundable ticket."

The next morning I had to check out by 10:00 a.m., but my flight wasn't leaving until 11:00 p.m. I thought maybe I should stay in town until it was time for my flight, but I figured I had spent enough money—$1,000 just for the room. I wasn't really thinking straight, either. I hadn't slept in ten days, what with the toilets flushing every twenty minutes, and my once-a-day diet of Subway sandwiches didn't help either, so I headed off for a long day at the airport. The airport was very small; all of about twenty-five yards. After reading pretty much everything in the airport, I went to the bar and talked to the bartender. I was the only person in the airport. I asked her, "Why do you live up here when it's so expensive?"

She answered, "I love it here and would work as many jobs as possible to continue living here. During the day, I'm a hairdresser, and I work as a bartender for a few hours a day. You have to go now, though, because it's time to close."

Damn, I had another six hours until my flight left.

For the next six hours I just sat in the airport and talked to the two attendants at the check-in windows. We were the only three people there. After a while, they bought me coffee and some potato chips.

Finally, as it got close to 11:00 p.m., I asked them, "Is the flight on time?"

"Sorry, we forgot to tell you," one said, "There's a blizzard in Edmonton so your flight will be delayed."

Forgot to tell me? I'm the only person here. I should have said screw it and stayed another night, but I was worried about my connecting flight. About midnight, the plane showed up. The woman doing security was the bartender; I guessed this was her third job.

There were two of us on the 747, which was another reassuring event. The flight attendants gave us all kinds of food. When we got to Edmonton, we were let off the plane in the middle of a runway. We both walked to the main terminal in the blizzard. It was about 2:00 a.m., and my connecting flight left at 6:00 a.m. The airport gave me a ten-dollar voucher and a room in a town nearby. We got in a van and went to the hotel. The driver said he would be back at 5:00 a.m. to pick us up for our flight. I tried to get some sleep but that didn't work because by that time, I had about an hour before the van was due back.

The next morning when I entered the airport, I immediately started to sweat, and my hands started to shake. My eyes were really red, but I had tried to make myself look presentable, since I usually get raked over the coals at airports. When I went through security, the guard said, "Rough night?" Oh, I knew this wasn't going to be a good day. After that, I filled out my customs card, not too legibly, and waited in line for my flight.

When I got to the front of the line, the two people in front of me looked as bad as I did, but all they said to the agent was, "We write cartoons," and they were let through right away.

When it was my turn, I was asked, "Are you on any medication or have you been taking drugs?"

"No, I was up in Yellowknife, and I couldn't sleep because of the toilets."

The agent looked at my customs card. "Why did you only buy a T-shirt and a license plate? That is a strange combination."

"Well?"

She looked at me again, but then said, "Just go," as I was holding up the line.

I swear that if it hadn't been for the blizzard, I would have been arrested or at least detained.

I was in the emergency exit row on the plane, and the door kept leaking water on my leg. I nudged the guy next to me. "Do you think I should say something about this?"

He looked startled. "Hell, yeah!"

"Stewardess," I said, "the emergency exit is leaking water."

She thanked me for telling her, but I didn't see her again for the rest of the flight.

We got to Philadelphia at about 10:00 p.m. I got my stuff and headed off for my truck. The weather wasn't too bad in Philly, but someone had stolen the mulch out of the back of my truck. It took about an hour to get home.

The next day a co-worker, that lives next door saw me and said, "You know some people were worried about you because they didn't know where you were. You also know that you have to leave a contact number before break just in case something happens."

I understood his concern because while I was in Yellowknife I tried to find the most obscure post cards and sent them to random people at work. I thought it was amusing, others didn't.

The rest of the school year went pretty smoothly; I set myself on cruise control until after exams. Usually, after spring break, most teachers just wanted the year to end. I always isolated myself to keep under the radar. This worked for close to seventeen years. Then it backfired.

Chapter 6
Hawaii

In the summer of 1994, John and I decided to drive in my truck to Los Angeles and fly to Hawaii. Much of the scenery in the Midwest is mundane, and in the summer, it's really hot, but the people were always hospitable. We camped the entire way and cooked the same kind of food that we had cooked on our drive to Alaska. This time, we ate a lot more buffalo meat at diners and restaurants than we had before. Most of the time, I thought it was just a spicy hamburger and that they called it buffalo so they could charge more.

We stopped at as many national parks as we could, including Custer National Park in Wyoming, which we thought was boring at first. The park is known for its buffalo and because part of *Dances with Wolves* was filmed there.

I said to John, "This is bull. All I've seen so far is a ram."

Then we went around the corner, and there must have been three hundred buffalo roaming around. Both of us said, "Wow!" and we watched people get out of their cars and take pictures of each other as they stood by the buffalo.

I looked at John and said, "Idiots," and we drove off.

The next national park we went to was Yellowstone. There had just been a major forest fire there, so there wasn't a lot to see but we did stop at Old Faithful, which I thought was a disappointment. I said, "You know, this is nothing like Bugs Bunny."

"What the hell are you talking about?" John asked.

"I mean it's built up to be a bigger deal than it actually is. I'm not impressed. At least in Bugs Bunny cartoons it was a lot bigger."

After that, we went to the Grand Canyon, which was impressive. We stayed at a KOA campground outside of the park and snuck in before the park opened so we wouldn't have to pay. John's a little more brave with the heights thing than I am. "Hey, let's get this guy to take our picture as close to the edge as possible," he suggested.

"You can do it, but I'm out of it. You know I don't like heights."

"All right, we'll compromise. We'll stand *here*." He pointed to a spot that was about three feet from the edge, and we found a guy to take the picture.

Then we crossed the Hoover Dam on our way to Burbank, California. We had to stop there so John could use the restroom. As he was doing his business, I looked at the dam. There were about two thousand people there.

It was impressive but not to the extent that I would make a specific trip to that destination. We continued to travel up and down Route 1 in California, stopping at Monterey.

"John, did you know that this was where the Monterey Pop Festival took place? My brother told me about it years ago. It was a three-day concert in June 1967."

"So what? I was one and what were you? Two months?"

"No, six months. But it was a big deal. My brother Mike told me about it. He said that The Jimi Hendrix Experience, Janis Joplin, Otis Redding, and The Animals were there. Eric Burdon and the other members of The Animals wrote a song called 'Monterey' after the festival." After talking about it, I couldn't get that song out of my head for two days.

"If you know so much about all this stuff," John said, "why don't you go into music?"

"Because I have no talent in that kind of thing. I know some facts but not enough to make a career out of it." When we got back in Burbank, we went to a travel agent to get our plane tickets.

I said, "We need tickets to Honolulu as soon as possible."

She just looked at us. "Just like that? No plans? Nothing?"

"No, we just drove in from Pennsylvania and want to see what Hawaii is like."

"All right, it'll take a few minutes. Do you want the emergency exit seats?"

"Yes."

That night, we stayed in Los Angeles, and the next day I parked my truck in long-term parking. I wasn't real comfortable about that at LAX since I'm not used to big cities and it didn't seem like a safe area. The flight was to be five or six hours, depending on the tailwind. We sat right across the aisle from the flight attendants and told them about our schools, which sounded great when we talked about it, even though we knew it was a crock. The flight attendants thought we were saints and gave us food from first-class.

Once we got to Honolulu, we tried to find a place to camp. Since we had our equipment and had read that you could camp on the beaches for two dollars a day, that was our only plan. We went around the entire island, but all of the campgrounds and beaches were closed. We didn't know what was up, so we went to the government building to find out. It was the same building as was shown in *Hawaii Five-0*. The inside was a huge empty hall—it was amazing—and there were offices jutting off of the main hallway. Finally, someone told us that the beaches and campgrounds on the entire island closed down for two days a week so that they could be cleaned and that we just happened to be there at that time.

John and I were determined to find a cheap place to stay, so we drove around the island again to find the cheapest place. After close to five hours, John said, "Screw this. I'll just put it on my credit card," and we ended up at the airport again, for $140 for the night.

The next day we walked around Waikiki, which is way overrated, as far as I'm concerned. For lunch, we stopped at a Popeyes, where a really drunk Hawaiian guy came up to me and started yelling, "You Irish! You Irish!"

After he yelled at me a number of times, I finally said, "Yes, I know I'm Irish."

Then the manager came over and kicked him out.

"What the hell was that?" I asked.

John said, "You got me."

From there we went to check out the volcanoes and walked as close as we could to the lava from a recent eruption. John wanted to cross the safety barrier to get closer, but we had read that sometimes the ground gave out right next to the lava, and there was a strong possibility it could kill the person who stepped on it, so we just wandered around. We went down a slope of hardened lava to a small town, which smelled like marijuana—it wasn't surprising; everyone was smoking pot.

"Aren't you worried that the police might arrest you?" John asked.

"No, they're too afraid to come down here since they think it's dangerous," one man replied.

"And why are these houses so nice in a semi-rundown area?"

"All of us have volcano insurance, so any time we get hit by lava, we just build nicer and nicer houses."

After exploring the volcano, we found a quiet place to camp on the beach. We watched a boy and a girl for most of the afternoon as they caught crabs with a long pole with claws on the end. Then we ate our dinner, which consisted of mangos. That night, there was a lot of noise over at the pavilion next to where we were camping, so we went over to check it out. There were about five big Hawaiian guys there, drinking and playing the ukulele. One said, "Do you two want some dried fish and fruit? It's like your popcorn or chips."

We gratefully accepted—and it actually was good. We hung out with them—until they tried to make us sing and play the ukulele. I said, "Sorry, neither of us can sing or play. It's late, and we have an early morning. Thanks, though." Then we went to bed.

The next day John went swimming while I sat in the sun.

He asked, "Aren't you going swimming?"

"No, I don't feel like it."

"Who the hell goes to Hawaii and doesn't go in the water?"

"John, these are the only shorts I have, and I don't feel like spending the rest of the day sitting in the sun, trying to dry them off."

The following day we went to the airport to see if we could puddle-jump to another island. We wanted to hit all of them but financially, we knew that wouldn't work. We also knew that the island of Niihau was only for the natives, and we weren't allowed on that island. For forty-five dollars each, we booked a flight to Maui. We were disappointed—everything was the same and somewhat boring. I was talking to my sister Sheila after the trip and mentioned that I didn't like Hawaii as much as I liked Alaska. She pointed out how lucky I was to have been to both Alaska and Hawaii within a couple of summers, something not many people were able to do. She was right, but then, most people wouldn't do it the way I did it.

Now, I was glad to be going home, even though it would take about a week to drive back from Los Angeles. We got our usual emergency-exit seats and tried to talk up the flight attendants again, hoping for the food from first class—and it worked.

As we were talking, I asked, "What's downstairs in the plane, where you prepare food?"

"There are microwave ovens, heaters for the food, and a rest area for us," one said. "You two can come down once we land, and we'll show it to you."

"Fran, what do you think?" John asked. "I'd like to see it."

"I'd like to see it, too, but it's getting late, and I'm worried about my truck and finding a place to stay."

As we were waiting for our bags after we landed, we heard an announcement in the terminal that our flight had been one of those targeted by the Unabomber, and they didn't tell us because they didn't want anyone freaking out.

That night, we drove around L.A., looking for a hotel. We stopped at a liquor store to get beer. The store had bulletproof glass between the customer and the attendant. After paying we grabbed the stuff and left. After about an hour of more driving, we found a place to stay that was in our price range.

The following day we started out for Pennsylvania, staying at most of the same places that we'd stayed at on the way to Los Angeles. By this time, John and I were starting to get on each other's nerves, so we didn't talk much. I also wasn't feeling all that great—my tent would get hot as hell, and it was difficult to sleep. We did stop in Las Vegas and played the slots for a little while. Neither of us is good, so it wasn't as exciting for us as it would have been if we'd been winning. From there, we went to Wyoming, where I took my first shower. Then it was on to Moab, Utah—nice but really hot. John took pictures of the stone arches that are prevalent in Utah as we camped in the desert and, ironically, it rained.

After that we continued east across Utah. We knew we had to find a hotel that night to dry out the tents, so we ended up in a small town that was having a rodeo that night. I wasn't really in the mood for a rodeo, but I had never been to one so I reluctantly agreed to go. It turned out to be a great time. Everyone was drinking, and the little kids ran into the rodeo with little pokers with different ribbons on them and ran after calves, sticking the calves with them. The calves were kicking the crap out of the kids, but the kids just kept getting up and would run after the calves again. Then the main attractions came, with the bulls and lassoing. It was great. After that we went into town, which was having a block party and snuck through the back of a bar to avoid the cover charge. We had waited until someone came out and grabbed the door. I started to talk to this really drunk girl that had a great body. One of the guys at the bar said, "She's the town slut, and you're in."

She asked, "Where are you coming from?"

"Hawaii."

"Don't you have to cross the ocean for that? Where are you going now?"

"I'm going home to Pennsylvania."

"Isn't that in that direction?" she asked, as she pointed east. Intelligence isn't at the top of my criteria for a one-night stand but her Marty Feldman eyes kind of bothered me, so I bagged it and went out into the street to hang out.

Chapter 7
Back Again and Mexico

The next day we took off and drove east. We had about a week before school started again and we had to get our classrooms set up. In my classroom, I had put up Holocaust pictures, but the administrator had complained that they were depressing and asked me to take them down—he didn't want pictures that showed dead people. Parents also complained that the pictures were too graphic. I'd been teaching an elective World War II class at the time. I couldn't teach about World War II without covering the Holocaust. It would be like teaching about the Civil War and not mentioning slavery. Still, I had to decide how to set up my classroom without the Holocaust pictures.

When I got back to school, I cleaned up my classroom and added some plants and new posters. John taught science and had left a few days before to do the same thing in Connecticut.

That year, the academic administrator told me that he couldn't stand walking by my room in the morning and seeing me with my feet on the desk. So he wouldn't see me, he ordered me to reconfigure my room. "Fix it," he demanded, "because it bugs me."

Man, lighten up, I thought, but I did it anyway. I moved my desk diagonally to the other side of the room so he couldn't see me.

This same administrator would sneak out the back door in the middle of the day and go home. Many times, he would e-mail us from his home about something he wanted us to accomplish within the next couple days. He was the only faculty member who had access to the school computers from home. Then, when people would complain he wasn't there to deal with it, his secretary would say that he had an appointment.

My classes always went fairly well, and I never really had any personal problems with the students, but the academic administrator, no matter who it was, always found something wrong. He or she did that with many of the teachers, except for those that kissed up the best, and I was terrible at doing that—I just didn't care enough to kiss up.

One day I was hanging out during my first period, a free period. I had corrected all of my homework and was just waiting for my second period. A few days before I had received an e-mail from the academic administrator telling me, "Fran, you can't wear work boots to school because it is difficult to enforce the dress code if the teachers aren't following it."

I thought, *Damn, that was last year that I wore work boots, and how the hell did he know?* I found out later that a kid named Paul had mentioned my name when he got caught wearing boots. I didn't think much of it; I felt the school had larger problems to worry about than what kind of shoes I was wearing.

Phil was a new full-time English teacher who I had been a cottage faculty with. Another English teacher had fought for Phil to get the job, but it turned out that Phil wasn't very good. He never completed or corrected the assignments, and the teacher that fought for him was a little embarrassed that he had recommended Phil for the job.

One day, at about ten or fifteen minutes into class, Phil still hadn't arrived. The academic administrator had to come down to unlock his door and let the kids in. At that moment, Phil walked through the hallway doors and said, "Thanks," and walked into the room.

The administrator didn't say anything to Phil; instead, he walked into my classroom and said, "I heard you are wearing boots to school, and that's inappropriate."

"No, I'm not," and showed him my swayed shoes.

I was wearing shoes that day, and I thought, *Damn, is this what it's come down to? Phil is late for class—in fact, he's late all the time—but this guy's only concern is if I'm wearing boots?* Soon, John and I started to make plans for the 1995 Christmas break; we decided to give Mexico a try. The first problem we ran into was in San Antonio— actually, it was more fun than a problem. I was driving my truck; we were getting hungry, so we stopped at a restaurant. I hadn't realized that the South was still so segregated. It was an Afro-American restaurant, and John and I were the only white people. It didn't bother me, but we did get some strange looks. John eventually had go to the bathroom which almost made the night worse and when he came back I thought we might have a problem, he had used the women's restroom. When he came back to the bar, a big Afro-American guy was holding his collar, and the guy said, "Does this belong to you?" Then everyone laughed.

John explained, "They were cleaning the bathrooms, and the doors were open, I didn't know which was which so I just went in."

We hung out there for a few hours, talking to a guy who was ninety-two and was planning to marry the twenty-five-year-old girl that was with him. He asked, "What are you two doing for Christmas? Do you want to come over to our house for dinner?"

"Thanks, but we don't really know what we are doing for Christmas. We want to get as far south into Mexico as possible before we have to head northeast again."

"Okay, the offer is open. Here's my number and I want to give you this." He signed a couple two-dollar bills and handed one to each of us. Then he and his girlfriend left.

"John, that was a little weird. It was funny, but weird. I wouldn't mind hanging out with them for Christmas."

"No, we have a plan. We have to get as far south as possible."

"What's the big deal, we only have a week and half left?"

"No, we have to go south."

"John, we never have a plan, why not stay here?"

"I don't want to, lets go back to the campground."

On the way back to the KOA, I was going way too fast, and the road was in bad shape. We hit a number of bad potholes at about 80 mph and blew out a tire. We stopped at a parking lot to change the tire, thinking everything was all right, and then drove to our site. We woke up at about 2:00 a.m., and I went out to take a look at the truck. One of the other tires had a huge bulge in it and was about to pop. We got in and tried to find a gas station that was open all night. Everything had bars on the windows. It almost felt like a scene from *Escape From New York*. We drove around for hours, until the sun came up, and ended up at National Tire Warehouse. The people working there were great. The guy who fixed my truck was familiar with where I lived. He said, "I was just in King of Prussia last week for a conference, and it seems like a nice place. Do you guys want to borrow my car to get something to eat?"

We thanked him, but decided and walked to a Mexican restaurant down the street. The repair only took a few hours and was fairly cheap. Right after we got my truck fixed, we went to visit the Alamo. I tried to find a parking spot, but there weren't any, so John got out and took pictures while I kept driving around the Alamo.

After that we headed south to Brownsville to cross the border. We had no problem at the border, but once we were crossed into Mexico, a bunch of guys started running after the truck. John said, "They only want money; keep on going."

We looked at all the crosses beside the road, at least I did since I was driving. I was a little concerned since there were so many. I wondered who could drive at night here. There weren't any street lights and the chickens and cows crossed the street at will. It seemed like a lot of people died on this road.

Finally, we hit the border of another Mexican state and I have no clue which one. As a history teacher I almost find it odd. Mexico is right down there and, for the most part, I know nothing about it and pretty much can care a less. When we hit the next state a guard started yelling at us in Spanish. Neither of us knew enough Spanish to understand the guard. All I knew was that he had bad breathe and needed to trim his nose hair. I had heard about people who got into trouble in foreign countries and spent years in jail. I didn't want that. Finally, we realized that the guard wanted a pass that we were supposed to get when we crossed the border. We realized then that the guys who had been running after the truck were probably trying to sell us passes.

John said, "We didn't know that we needed a pass." Fortunately, the guard sent us back to the border to get a pass instead of arresting us.

"John, my nerves are pretty shot. I just want to get out of Mexico."

"All right, but be good when we get to the border."

When we got to the border, the attendant asked how long we had been in Mexico, and I made a bonehead move and said, "Only a few hours."

"Pull over," he said. The border officers climbed throughout the truck and checked all of our luggage. Then the drug-sniffing dogs were sent in. "Okay, clean up your stuff and get the hell out of here."

I said to John in a low voice, "Let's just go and find some place to stay."

John and I finally found a place to stay with a kitchenette and a pull-out bed that John slept on. We got new clothes because mine were a wreck again. John wanted to go out, but I had enough for the day and stayed in. He came back a couple hours later and said, "That was a great time. You should have come."

The next day we kept seeing signs for a steak restaurant. They read: "If you finish this fifty-ounce steak, it's free." Every time we passed another of the signs, John would say, "I'm going to do it. I'm going to do it."

I kept thinking, *You're going to puke. You're going to puke.*

We found a KOA a few miles from the steakhouse and drank a few beers; then John said, "I'm ready; let's go."

At the steakhouse there were awards on the wall of all the people who had finished the fifty-ounce steak. John said, "I can do it." After paying his fifty dollars, the waitress put us at a special table at the center of the restaurant, with a TV camera from Holland focused on us. I ordered rattlesnake, and it did taste like chicken but really boney. John, however, didn't anticipate the pitfalls of the challenge. He got the fifty-ounce steak, but he also got the salad, appetizer, and corn that came with it—and he had to finish everything within an hour.

"John, you're never going to be able to do it."

"Thanks for the support. Shut up." He started to eat as fast as he could.

"All right, but you are starting to make me sick, so I'm going into the other room for a beer."

He mumbled, "Loser," with his mouth full of lettuce. We hadn't been eating much on our trip, so our stomachs had shrunk, and John was in for a bad night.

About twenty minutes later, John joined me in the bar. "I couldn't do it," he admitted. "Let's go."

In the parking lot, he keeled over and threw up. I knew he would; it was a fifty-dollar puke.

The next night we went to Corpus Christi and stayed there for the night. The windows of our room had bullet holes in them, but by that point, it didn't bother me—I had stayed in plenty of hotels with bullet holes in them. I did have a problem, though, with the bedding. I didn't want to sleep on the sheets—they were dirty and even too nasty for me.

The next day we headed to Houston for Christmas and set up at the local KOA. The KOA was surprisingly busy for Christmas. We splurged and got a cabin. That night, we had a few beers, and then John asked what I wanted to do for dinner. We decided to go to an IHOP that was near the freeway. We had waffles and sausage and then went back to our cabin.

On the last night of our trip we stopped outside Wheeling, West Virginia. Nothing against the people of West Virginia, but Wheeling is a pit. We stayed at a campground outside of town, and it just stunk like stagnant water. We set up camp and made our usual cowboy stew. That was the highlight of the night. The next day we headed back to Downingtown.

Chapter 8
Costa Rica and Ecuador

The rest of the year was uneventful for the most part, and John and I thought about what we were going to do that summer. By this time we had decided that if we were going north, I would drive to Connecticut and if we were going south, he would drive to Pennsylvania. We had pretty much exhausted everything in the United States, and we had hit every country, state, territory, and province in North America; at least I had. John had been to close to forty countries more than I had, but he still wanted to visit smaller, out-of-the-way places. That was fine with me. I didn't want to go to populated areas full of tourists. I didn't want to see Americans; I wanted to see everything else.

That summer we decided to go to Costa Rica and Ecuador, planning to spend two weeks in each. One reason we wanted to go to Costa Rica was because one of my former students, Luke, had inherited land in the rain forest from his father. Apparently, his father had been arrested a number of times for growing pot. Luke was nothing like his father; he was a strict vegetarian and lived a pathetically clean life. I had known Luke for close to eight years by this point; he was a nice kid.

In his senior year, he and a number of the other seniors came up to me and asked, "Mr. Finn, wouldn't a cruise be a good time?"

"No, I hate that stuff."

"Come on, we need an adult, and Henry's mom is a travel agent. We can get a great deal."

"No."

"Come on. If we get another teacher to go, will you?"

"If it's someone I don't mind hanging out with I'll think about it." I figured no one would say yes.

A couple hours later they came back and said, "Mr. Sampson said he would go. He's a good guy. How about now?"

"Oh, all right. How much will it cost?"

"Eight hundred dollars."

"Eight hundred dollars for a stupid cruise? That's a lot of money."

"Come on, Mr. Finn; it'll be a good time."

"All right, but you guys better be good, and I'm not taking any responsibility for anything you do wrong."

"Okay, that's fine with us."

We had to drive to Florida to begin the cruise. I had driven to Florida a number of times and knew it was a long trip and even longer by bus, which was how I would be traveling. The old lady in the seat next to me fell asleep on my shoulder, and after the first ten hours, I was already sick of the trip. We stopped once for gas, and then again in Fayetteville, North Carolina, where we were to get a connecting bus to Tampa. The driver for the connection, however, wasn't there, and to make the cruise, we had to get on a bus within the next hour. Fortunately, someone found a driver, and we headed to Tampa.

Once we got on the ship, a photographer took our pictures and hung them up in the hallway on the way into the reception area. Then we went to our rooms.

"I know we are supposed to have an adult in each room to have an authority figure, but that would kind of stink for all of us since it would be boring for you guys to have me looking over your shoulders," I said.

"Pat, I'm going to stay in this room with Phil and three other kids, but that room is in my name so don't mess it up or I'll get charged." Luckily, they didn't, and they got the rugby players next door to them to get them alcohol, so they were drunk most of the time, and Pat hooked up with some girl that looked to be twelve.

The cruise line had two stops where they boarded more passengers. At each stop, the captain told the new people that they had to be on deck at a certain time, with their life jackets on, so that we could go over the emergency process.

It seemed to me that most of the women on the cruise were either in college or about my age and married to a guy in his sixties or seventies. I knew I wasn't going to meet any eligible women in the next seven days and figured I'd make the best of it. The first thing Phil and I did was get something to drink. Phil isn't a big drinker, but I wanted a beer—at eight dollars, I knew I wouldn't be buying many beers while on the cruise.

Our cabin was on the inside of the ship because it was cheaper, and it was dark. In the cabin with me and Phil were the kids who didn't want to party with the other kids: Luke, Tim, and Mark. Phil was the first one in and chose the single bed. Two bunk beds were left. Luke grabbed the upper bunk of one bunk, and Tim grabbed the lower bunk. The other bunk was for Mark and me. Mark said, "I have bad knees so I can't climb to the top bunk."

"Bad knees? How can you have bad knees? You're only in high school." Still, I took the top bunk. I tried out the bed, and it was pretty small.

That night, everyone was allowed to go to the dining center to meet the captain; we would be eating there each night. We were allowed to go to dinner dressed as we were when we boarded, but we decided to get dressed up a little anyway. The food was really good, but I am more of a McDonald's kind of guy. After that night, I decided that I would eat on the lower deck, where it was more casual. Luke followed suit. I guess a guy who decides to live in the rain forest really isn't that kind of person either.

Right after dinner, Phil went back to the room and fell asleep. That became his rhythm for the rest of the trip. At first, I was kind of bummed that Phil didn't stay awake so we could hang out together, but these were good kids and they didn't mind my being with them; sometimes, I just went off on my own. That first afternoon, I saw everything there was to see on the ship. I checked out the nude sunbathing area (I was fully clothed), but it was too cold for anyone to be nude. I checked that out a number of times, but never saw any nude sunbathers.

That night, after I'd gone to bed, the ship tipped to about a forty-five degree angle. It scared the hell out of me and Luke—the other guys were still out—but Phil just rolled against the wall and never woke up. The glasses fell off the desk and our clothes went flying everywhere. I jumped out of bed and ran out the door to see what was happening. The only other person in the hallway was an older woman who was looking out her door. We looked at each other and then went back into our rooms. The next day, I asked Pat, who'd been out on deck when the ship tipped, how it felt to him.

"We didn't even notice that the ship tipped," he said. "Some people fell down, but we just figured they were drunk."

By the middle of the next day I had pretty much exhausted everything I wanted to do on the ship, so I decided to go to the gym and lift. I was disappointed by the weight room. It was really small, and there wasn't a decent bench and no squat rack. There weren't any dumbbells over fifty pounds. I thought, *Damn, I paid a lot for this trip, and this is the stuff they give me.* Then I started lifting and realized right away why that stuff wasn't there. Because the boat was constantly moving, keeping my balance was really hard.

Later that morning, we were dropped off at Cancun. We had to be back by 5:00 p.m., so that gave us six hours to explore Cancun. We walked around for a while, and because I've been collecting weapons for years, I bought a Mexican machete. One of the kids, Gary, bought Cuban cigars, and the kids smoked as many as they could before we had to be back to the ship.

That night, Phil and everyone else wanted to go to a karaoke cigar-smoking bar. I hate karaoke, and I don't smoke. That's a strange combination anyway. You'd think everyone would have to be drunk to do karaoke. I used to tell the kids that my voice is so bad that I don't even sing in the shower, but that wasn't entirely true. I never was a big shower singer but I used to try to tick off my college roommates and my dog by singing off key. Smoking was at least one vice I haven't picked up. I went along with them anyway, mostly because I was bored and even though I don't smoke I like the smell of cigars which technically means I might as well be smoking. My brothers are into that and even have their own cigar clippers, if they're called that. Whenever they smoked I put in a huge chew.

At the bar, Phil signed us all up to do a song.

"Phil, there is no way I'm getting up there," I said. "You and the kids can do it but if you call me up, I'm walking out."

The kids thought it was great and seemed to have a good time. After that, Phil went to bed, but the kids and I went to a comedy show. I bought the kids a couple of beers a piece and then thought I would walk out to go to bed but before I could a woman left for the bathroom and the comic started to make fun of her so I figured I'd wait it out. I had been through that in college and the comics are relentless.

The next day, the captain told us that we would be passing by Cuba, and if we wanted to see it, we should go to the stern. I was pretty sure I would never get to travel there, so I went to the stern and waited. Four hours later, the captain said that we had bypassed Cuba because of inclement weather. I was ticked off but figured I was four hours closer to getting off that ship.

When we finally reached Tampa again, we had to go through customs, where the agents were spot-checking people. I put my duffle bag through the metal detector. The officer said, "Oh, you bought a machete," and he let me through.

Gary was next. The agent said, "You have Cuban cigars. Do you know they are illegal in the United States?"

"No," Gary responded.

"Well, I'll have to confiscate them."

After we got through customs, I turned to Gary and said, "You're such a liar. You know they are illegal."

"Well, I wasn't going to tell him that."

"It's stupid anyway," I said. "I get through with a weapon, and you can't get through with cigars. That trade embargo needs to end."

We took the bus back to Philly, Phil's hometown. His father has lived there his entire life and tried to drive us back to Downingtown, but we got lost in Philly. I thought, *How do you get lost in a city where you've lived your entire life?* Then I thought, *I've lived here for a long time, and I don't know anything about the area.* I did know that I was damn glad the trip was over and that I would never go on another cruise the rest of my life.

After that year, Luke went on to Arizona State and graduated with a degree in education. After looking for jobs in the United States, he decided to take over his father's land in Costa Rica. He invited me down for a visit and I told him I was bringing a friend.

When we landed in San Jose, it was really hot. Once we got through customs, we headed out to the street. Luke was right there waiting for us, and he had a long beard.

I said, "Nice face."

John said, "What the hell are you doing? You're going to get us killed!" He hadn't recognized Luke from the pictures I had shown him from school and thought I was making rude comments to a stranger.

Luke showed us around San Jose and helped us get our rental car. The car was in John's name because I had too many points on my license and wasn't able to get an international drivers license.

"I'm sorry I can't help you guys out more," he said, "but I don't know much about the city. I only come into the city every three months to check my e-mail."

"Did you get the e-mail that I sent last month?" I asked. "I wanted to know if they sell Copenhagen here."

"No and I have no clue."

Bringing chew into a country usually meant it would be confiscated, especially if I brought more than four tins—when my backpack went through the metal detector, security would think it was a bomb.

"Is the water safe to drink?" I asked.

"Fran, it's Central America," John said. "No, the water is not safe to drink."

"Yes, it is, sir," Luke replied.

"Okay, but don't call me sir. It makes me feel old," and Luke led us to our hotel.

He described his road trip through the Central American countries and some problems he ran into in Nicaragua. "The major thing I have to say is do not go out at night because I've heard the city is very dangerous. Here, I'll draw you a map on how to get to my ecolodge in the rain forest. Okay, when you get to the big tree on the left, turn left."

Later that day, we went downstairs to the hotel bar to eat and started talking to a guy from Colorado who said he had been there for three months but hadn't left the city because it was dangerous. Damn, we planned on seeing the entire country. He said, "Have you seen the traffic? It's crazy? I can't navigate through that."

I replied, "Yeah, it reminds me of Ted Nugent's song *Free For All*."

He laughed and agreed. The traffic was nuts; no one followed the road signs, if there were any. The roads were in bad shape and most of the manholes didn't have covers on them.

That night we decided to walk around town anyway. Right outside the hotel there was a prostitute who asked in a deep voice, "How about some of this?" As we kept walking, she yelled, "What? Are you guys gay?"

"No, we don't think you're a woman." We continued to a dive bar.

We only stayed for a little while because the people were a little weird. They had a lot of tattoos and piercings all over their bodies. Most of them were Americans. We were trying to get away from Americans, but Costa Rica was riddled with them. On the way back to the hotel, John told me he thought it was a gay bar but didn't tell me while we were there because he knew that would bother me. We also ran into the prostitute again, but this time she was busy giving a guy a hand job at the red light.

The next day we left to try to find Luke's ecolodge. I was glad because I couldn't get Dionne Warwick's song about San Jose out of my head. I didn't really know the song and why I knew the few words I did, I don't know. What helped was being preoccupied with not sliding off the side of a muddy, wet mountain. We filled up the tank and headed off to the rain forest. It was Luke's birthday, so we bought a lot of beans, vegetables, and a couple cases of beer. The Costa Rican people were pretty poor, so a group of kids followed us back to the car because they couldn't believe how much money we spent. The rain forest was amazing, but the roads were dangerous—they were actually dirt trails, which were muddy with a shit load of potholes. Most of the time we were driving on a cliff, and it seemed like we would just topple over.

I said, "Look for a big tree on the left? All the trees are big."

"All right, Fran, we can only drive until we hit half a tank, so we can make it back out." Then, in the middle of nowhere, we found a bar.

"I'm going in to ask someone for directions," John said. "You stay here to keep an eye on the car." A few minutes later John returned. "I couldn't understand the guy, even with my phrase book, so we have to get the hell out of here,"

We e-mailed Luke, telling him we couldn't find his ecolodge. We knew he wouldn't get the e-mail for another three months, when he went back to San Jose.

From there we tried to find a place to stay. We drove into the forest again and up a steep dirt road. A car in front of us had died, and the truck that was towing it used a long branch as its tow. We didn't see any chains; it was kind of strange. We drove for a few hours, up and down the dirt roads, and finally we came to a deep stream that crossed the road.

"Fran, what do you think we should do?" John asked. We got out of the car to take a look.

"The car is in your name and under your insurance, so I don't care."

"Hey, we agreed: everything 50/50. We can't turn back, and I haven't seen any other roads, so let's try to get across the stream. I'll just back up and floor it."

"I'll go with that."

It was a process that seemed almost in slow motion. I looked out my window, and the water was halfway up the window and leaking onto my pants. I thought we were going to be swept away, but it was only a minute or so before we crossed the stream.

We finally came across some rental bungalows by the ocean and stopped to find out how much they cost. We were trying to find places under thirty dollars a night; fifteen dollars each would be fine. This place was twenty dollars, so we stayed. I think we were the only people there. I was surprised and pleased to find that our bungalow even had a flush toilet.

There were no walls on the bungalow, just mosquito netting. There was a central dining area but we didn't eat there; we just had beef jerky. The owner came over to show us the screaming monkeys, which were everywhere. Then we went down to the beach to see if we could find any sea turtles, as there was a sea turtle research center right up the beach. We didn't see any, but I went swimming to clean off. Other than the owner and his daughter, we didn't see another person the entire time we were there.

The next day we headed down the other side of the mountain to a resort town. As John drove, I looked at the houses, which were really small. They were big enough for a bed, a chair, and a stove. I don't know if they had bathrooms, but they must have because I didn't see any outhouses. Both of the doors were open because it was so hot, so we could see inside the houses, and they looked really clean. A lot of them were for sale and cost about two thousand dollars. I said, "You know, I could afford that, but the heat would kill me."

We found a place to stay for about thirty dollars a night and decided to stay two days because we had seen most of the country already and still had days to go. We got a couple of hamburgers and a case of beer and then sat in front of our room, watching the people. After two days, we were happy to leave because there were too many Americans and the water smelled really bad.

From there, we headed inland to a remote village. We talked to a guy from Switzerland who had moved to Costa Rica twenty years before, and he told us about how bad the crime was and that getting medical attention was expensive. He said that the only competent doctors were in San Jose, and that was a four-hour bus ride.

I asked, "Then why do you stay here?"

"Other than that, this place is great; laid back," he said. "Also, you guys need to watch out about the coconut trees. I know it sounds stupid, but I've seen it happen—I saw a guy get hit in the head by a falling coconut and it killed him, split his head right open."

The next day we went to the Atlantic side of the country. It was kind of cool, seeing the Atlantic and Pacific oceans within a day. We found a room for about twenty dollars that was semi-clean—except there were ants in the bed. There were also lizards in the room, but they were harmless. Other than scaring the hell out of me in the middle of the night when I went to the bathroom, they left me alone. We decided to spend two days there to waste time again, and we walked around town. The next morning the owner of the hotel showed us a sloth in a tree in the front of the hotel. I had never seen one up close. The sloth just stared back at us.

I always woke up hours earlier than John, and I felt reasonably safe walking around town at 4:00 a.m. A number of times I would run into the stragglers from the previous night who were often really drunk but amusing. I only had one encounter with a local. He came up to me on the beach as I watched the early-morning surfers and asked, "Do you have any money?"

I showed him my pockets and said, "All I have is this beer." I got up and walked back to my room, and he yelled after me, "I'm not going to mug you. I just need some money."

I kept going. After he left I went back to watching the surfers and started petting a stray dog that had come up to me. When the sun finally came up and I could see the dog more clearly, I found out it had no hair on the other side of its body. The next day, I had a rash all over my body. I stood in the sun, hoping that it would dry out my skin. I looked like a leper. I thought the airline might refuse to let me on the plane if I looked like this.

When the owner saw me she said, "Oh, my God!"

I knew I looked bad but I had to ride it out and hope the rash would be gone in a couple of days when we left for Ecuador.

That day we ate breakfast at this walk-in stand, which was great, and I looked forward to eating there again, but it was never open again. It was run by an older American guy who made great omelets. I asked a local guy, "Why isn't the omelet stand open?"

"Because if someone makes enough money in one day, he doesn't open up again until he needs money again."

"That sounds like a good life."

We also met a couple of high school kids who had been working at a sea turtle rescue mission for the summer—cocky kids from California. According to them, their parents forced them to volunteer for the summer, but they didn't like it, so one night they called a cab, left, and were riding out their time at the hotel until they figured out what to do. I never bothered to ask what they were actually volunteering for because I really didn't care. Then one of them started to give me tips on teaching.

I wanted to punch the kid. I said, "Shut up. You have no idea what you're talking about." I agreed that there is plenty of bullshit that kids learn in school, but each teacher and school is bound by the national standards, and that the state comes in every few years to make sure that the school is following the requirements; if it doesn't, the school loses its funding or is not accredited. Most people don't know this or understand it. I don't understand all of it and I taught for a long time so I wasn't willing to even try telling this kid.

From there, John and I headed a little north inland. We walked around town that night and hit a few bars. At one bar, I guess the waiter was getting frustrated because we weren't ordering anything to eat and said, "Would you like to try some ceviche?"

I replied, "Sure, why not?" and he came back with some seafood and something else that looked like it could be beef in a small dish.

John refused to eat. But I tried both and told John, "This stuff is disgusting," and we left.

That night we got some chicken and hung out in the room. John went to bed, and I stayed up watching the Jeffrey Dahmer movie while eating my chicken. All of a sudden, John yelled, "Turn that shit off and go to bed."

"What the hell was that? I'm just eating dinner?"

Then he got up and grabbed the keys to the car and said, "You know, I just might leave you here," and left.

I thought, *Shit, I've seen that mother get mad before and there's no telling what he'll do. He's taken off before and not come back for a long time, leaving me stranded. If he has his passport I can see him leaving.* So I looked for his passport and hid it.

He came back a few hours later, really drunk. The next morning I asked, "Do you remember last night?"

"No, but I had fun." After I recapped, he said, "Oh, I would never just take off."

I wasn't so sure, and then we got ready to leave. When we went outside, we found that we had a flat tire. We didn't even know where the spare tire was and had to ask the owner of the motel where to look, which wasn't easy because the guy spoke a mile a minute in Spanish. Finally, we just looked at him, and I guess he understood that we had no clue what he was talking about, so he just grabbed the tire iron out of John's hands and did it for us. We said thanks and left.

I didn't find out the significance of that night until years later when we were in Peru. I didn't even really worry about it that much. I knew he flew off the handle from time to time but if I had known what actually happened to him I wouldn't have been so insensitive. I didn't even know I was being insensitive at the time. Unknowingly I was an "unintentional dick." We came up with that term early in our travels on our way to Alaska. It's when a person is a dick but doesn't even realize they are being a dick until it is pointed out to them. When he finally did tell me I promised I would never tell anyone.

From there we were supposed to meet up with another teacher from my school, Diane, and her husband, who was a professor at the University of Pennsylvania. They were wealthy and stayed at the nicest places; John and I stayed at the cheapest places we could find. Diane's husband had wanted to go to Costa Rica to surf and asked us to come over.

That day, we tried to waste time by going to the beach, and I washed off again. Then we found a place to stay. It was a really great spot, and we had our own little building but the bed was infested with ants, more than I previously had experienced, which didn't make it easy to sleep. We watched *Passion of the Christ* in Spanish with the locals at the outside bar, as it poured down rain. Then I ordered some calamari and went to bed with the ants.

The next day we ate some hamburgers and went to look for Diane's hotel. We were amazed at how clean it was. They had two bedrooms, two bathrooms, and a loft for other people to sleep. The place was great, and Diane said, "I thought you guys might stay, so we got extra rooms."

John, who didn't know them, said, "Thanks, but if we don't experience what the real people experience, what's the point? I don't want to be a rich, snobby American and flaunt anything."

It was somewhat rude but I agreed, to a degree. I liked Diane's hotel; it had everything a person could want, even a private beach, but it wasn't "real." They were closed off from the rest of the world, and that turned me off.

The next day we had to head back to San Jose to catch our flight to Quito. The ride to the airport was difficult as usual, with numerous potholes and motorcycles doing whatever they felt like. I still had my rash but was hoping it wasn't as obvious as I knew it was. We waited at the terminal for an hour or so, and then started boarding.

The flight to Quito was laid-back, but Quito wasn't as nice as I thought it might be. It was winter in Ecuador, but at its lowest temperature it was about seventy degrees. We both were wearing shorts and T-shirts, but as we walked around, we looked at the local people in their heavy coats and scarves. They would point and laughed at our attire.

At the start of the trip, John realized as we were flying over Miami that he had left his ATM card on his kitchen table, and I had to lend him money. At first I didn't care because I knew he would pay me back, but by the end of the trip, somehow, I owed him money. I didn't know how that happened.

We needed to find a place to stay and grabbed some Club beer, which I think was nonalcoholic but the label was in Spanish, and we couldn't read it. Most of the places we found were hostels. That didn't bother me—I've slept in plenty of hostels—but I didn't like sharing a room with people I didn't know. We found a place on the main street, and we got a room in the back, hoping it would be reasonably quiet. It wasn't; people partied all night and a band went up and down the street on the back of a truck, playing music. Women (I presume they were prostitutes) were running up and down the hallways, screaming, and I could hear them in the rooms next door, making their money.

The next day I asked John, "Did you hear all that last night?"

"What? I didn't hear anything?"

"Geez, I wish I could sleep like you. You'd be a burglar's dream."

Sleeping was always a problem for me. The kids use to ask why I got up so early, and I would tell them the story: My family lived in a huge house, big enough that my two brothers and two sisters and I had our own rooms. We also had four bathrooms. I was, unknowingly, a spoiled kid. I didn't know any better; I figured everyone lived like I did. It wasn't until I moved to Pennsylvania that I realized how fortunate I'd been. When I was a kid, my father would go to bed at 8:00 p.m. and turn down the heat because heating a house that size was expensive. If we complained that it was getting cold, he'd reply, "Put a sweater on or go to bed." We usually chose going to bed, so waking up early wasn't a problem. My father's alarm went off at 4:00 a.m., so he could do rounds at the hospital. Then my mother would wake anyone who wasn't already up. We all had to take showers before school and since I was the youngest, I was last. That meant there was no hot water. My mother tried to reduce this to a minimum by either flushing the toilet or coming into the shower and shutting off the water saying, "You've been in there long enough." It didn't matter if we had soap in our hair; our time was up. The kids would say, "Mr. Finn, that's hard to believe, since we can go to bed whenever we want."

The next day we left for the equator at about 6:00 a.m. At least we thought it was the equator. It was labelled as the equator, but we found out later that it was just a symbol, and the equator was about fifty yards away. It was close enough for me. I had also heard that the water flushed down the toilet in the other direction and I wanted to see that. I really couldn't tell whether or not it did.

After that, we flew from Quito to Quenca. My rash was going away, so I felt a little better. The airport was really small—smaller than the one in Yellowknife—and we hung out and drank some beers. It just so happened that the president of Ecuador was there at the same time, but we never saw him, although we did see plenty of security and part of the army.

"Look Fran, all the soldiers are shorter than you."

"I get it John, I'm short. You can stop now."

We finally got on the plane. One of the passengers realized he was on the wrong flight and alerted the flight attendant. We were already on the runway and going at a pretty good clip. Apparently, they called the terminal and got a truck to drive alongside the plane. Then they opened up the plane door and lowered the guy onto the truck. I couldn't believe it. They didn't even stop, and no one seemed the worse for it.

After a forty-five-minute flight, we landed in Quenca. It seemed to be an ancient town with churches, at least one, on every street. John tried to find a place to stay, as I sat on top of the luggage and watched people, a lot of whom seemed to have disabilities. The worst was an old lady with a slab of thick skin over one of her eyes. A group of girls coming from school pointed and covered their mouths like they were gagging. I felt sorry for the lady; it wasn't her fault. I later found out that medical attention is not one of the top priorities in Ecuador.

John came back after about a half-hour, out of breath, and said, "I found a place. I think it's an old monastery. There are some dentist offices on the second floor, but we got a room on the third floor."

When we got there I said, "Wow, this place is big and the beds are great. Hey, you must not have checked out the bathroom." We realized that to sit on the toilet, we'd have to put our feet in the shower, and the toilet seat was really small. (I pride myself as a connoisseur of toilet seats).

"Why do you care?" John asked. "You never take showers, and we'll only be here a day or two."

That night we walked around town and stopped at a couple of churches to check them out. At every one, there were disabled people, begging for money. Then we stopped at a place to get hamburguesas, since that was the only word I came close to being able to pronounce. As we were eating we saw a woman walk by with a towel over her head; she was being led by each hand by two other women. I couldn't imagine how disfigured she must have been to hide her face with a towel after what I had already seen.

Later on we snuck some beers into the old monastery and went to bed. At about 2:00 a.m., I heard screeching from the field out back and said to John, "What the fuck do you think that is?"

"They're probably just slaughtering a pig for the market tomorrow."

"Are they doing it with a butter knife? It's been going on for about twenty minutes."

"Just try to sleep."

The following day we walked through the market, and there were about twenty slaughtered pigs, with the heads hanging right next to the bodies. In most of the countries I've been to, most of the meat is left out all day and infested with flies. I never felt very safe eating the meat in those countries. The vegetables weren't much better because the water used to clean off the vegetables wasn't clean. The people in these countries were used to it, but we always got sick.

The next day we went to the coast to Manta and stayed there for a few days. It was clean enough for us and cheap. We got a hotel room on the ocean and would go down to the restaurants to drink and eat. One place had great calamari. There, we ran into American naval men and hung out with them for a while. One of these guys was chewing, and I asked, "What are you chewing? I can't find chew anywhere."

"Right off the base I can buy Skoal for about twenty dollars."

"Twenty bucks? I don't want to spend that much. I've been recycling my Copenhagen."

"Can I have some?" he asked.

"I told you; it's recycled."

"I don't care. I can't stand Skoal but it's all I can get."

Even though I was running out, it's kind of an unwritten rule for chewers to share. "I only have a little, so don't take much. I only have a few days left and can buy more when I get to Miami."

After that we went to a city that we were told was just like Miami but it wasn't; it was kind of boring because there was really nothing there. We couldn't find a place to eat and ended up playing pool with a couple locals at a dive bar. We lost every time. The next day we flew out to Quito and stayed at a hotel across from the airport; we were leaving the following morning. We'd fly to Miami to Philadelphia and then home.

Chapter 9
Parent's Weekend and Seniors

The following year I got a little more responsibility. It was during Parent's Weekend. Parent's Weekend was always held three weeks into the school year. I thought that was stupid because I barely knew any of the kids' names by that point. The turnover at the school was usually about fifty percent so there were always new kids. We did get a list of students' parents who were coming, but it was never accurate. I would prepare for the parents that I was supposed to see, with the kid's grades for every assignment, along with a syllabus and a course outline, but then other parents would come in and say, "How's my son doing?" I didn't even know who they were. The parents wore name tags, but most of the time, the parents' names were different than their sons' names.

That year I had to apologize to the parents of one kid. The first day, this kid was off the wall and bouncing all over the place. He just couldn't stay in his seat. I finally said, "Are you ADD?" He was, so I apologized to the parents for asking him that, but they just laughed. "That's no big deal," his mother said. "He's just like that."

The new responsibility happened when I punched a student in the arm and his parents saw me. About five minutes later, the academic administrator came in, and I thought I was fired for sure. Then she asked, "Do you want to run mock trial?"

"Sure, I'd love to."

I wasn't even really sure what it was at the time. I had to go to a seminar with a local lawyer in West Chester to learn the procedure of a trial. He must have been really uptight because he hardly had any fingernails. At assembly, I made an announcement for sign-ups and got about twenty kids to sign up to do the mock trial. Once the material was sent to me, I handed it out—and everyone quit except for five kids. The material was about a hundred pages and was based on a real case. No one wanted to go over that much material. I could understand. They already had required sports until about 5:30 p.m., and then dinner at 6:00 p.m., and a required study hall from 7:30 p.m. to 9:30 p.m. Lights out were at 10:00 p.m. They had no free time.

After that, I had to find two lawyers to train the kids. The lawyers must have had to do it as community service because the kids treated them poorly. We met every Tuesday and Thursday nights from 7:00 p.m. until 9:00 p.m. We were lucky if everyone showed up. Some nights, we had two kids. They were there with their laptops and would send e-mails to me during this time, writing about how much they hated it. I knew we were going to get killed, and we did, because other local schools had full-time classes on this, and we only had a month to prepare.

Our first mock trial was against a school a town away, and we left early on a Wednesday so we could take a tour of the Chester County Court House and watch a DUI trial. A couple things happened when we got to the courthouse that I never even thought to address. The first thing was that when we were going through the metal detector, two of the kids on the team had knives. We were escorted to a separate room to fill out paperwork so they could get their knives back when we left. Then, when the trial started, one of the kids on the team started laughing at the man accused of the DUI charge. When he realized the entire courtroom was looking at us, he pulled his suit coat over his head which only made it worse.

During our competition, we lost every debate handedly, and the opposing coach said, "You're just like me; you're just doing this because you were told to." He was right.

Then, one of the mothers of a student on our team asked if one of the other kids had been smoking pot before the competition. "His eyes are half shut," she pointed out, "and he's speaking so slowly and softly."

"No, I used to think that, too, but I met his family, and everyone in his family is exactly the same."

To be eliminated from the mock trial tournament was to lose twice, which we did easily in the first two meets.

I did mock trial for three years and then started to ignore the messages from the state about the competitions. I was embarrassed to be seen with some of these kids because of the way they acted in public. It didn't seem like they had a filter for their actions or thoughts.

That learning experience continued with the senior trips although most were fun and I did learn some new skills, along with the politics of this particular school.

We did go to different areas every year for about the first ten years. At first this seemed like a great idea and it was. Plenty of the different areas were a great experience and the students didn't really bother me. They acted almost like I would have when I was their age. Maybe even like I do now when I'm in a different country that I know I'll never be visiting again; immature, a wise ass, disrespectful to a point, and almost belligerent. Most of the time they didn't understand what they had done wrong. Like I have in recent years and I'm way older than them. Certain behaviors are acceptable in different situations and I and they didn't realize we had done something unacceptable until it was already done.

We always gave them the history and atmosphere of the area we were about to visit and that they were representing the school but how many high school seniors actually listen to that. Most of the time they were thinking, as I was also, "Lets go, I'll deal with that stuff when I get there."

If someone keeps harping on a point, I tend to, as most, to turn off and nod as if to understand. Unless it's really important. I don't think most people will admit to this but I know it's there. I have run into it plenty of times. Stories I've retold as if for the first time, being misquoted and the misquote being taken as fact.

My first senior trip was to the Chesapeake Bay during Hurricane Fran where we took a forty-two-foot schooner out during the hurricane. Most of the kids and I had never been on one and hung on for our lives as the captain tried to scare the hell out of us by the way he was piloting the boat. The following year it was on to Coatesville, Pennsylvania where we watched a KKK rally from the distance and then participated in a biker wedding.

Throughout the years we went to the Grand Canyon in Pennsylvania to hike, Hawk Mountain in Pennsylvania for rock climbing, Jim Thorpe, Pennsylvania where we learned that the locals really hated our school and threatened to beat everyone up that night. The next day we went mountain biking and then kayaking down the Delaware River. It was then on to hiking a portion of the Appalachian Trial. Which personally, for me, was the worst since I wasn't in shape to hike that far. The final few years we went to a facility in New Jersey where the facilities facilitators took over and we were bystanders.

We all learned things through these experiences; some good some bad. We learned how to ration our food because those that didn't found ways to steal other's food. Who were the leaders, how to coexist in a different atmosphere, sharing, taking care of the sick, dealing with the authorities (Park Rangers, Police), stereotypes, people's weakness, perseverance, and kindness.

As for the politics of this particular school I had to type up a number of documents about the Senior Weekend so actions could be taken. Nothing was really done and I realized that it was mostly just paperwork that possibly would be put on file.

Not all of these experiences were enjoyable but usually those kinds of things aren't, but they are useful. Most people don't even realize how useful they were until years later.

Chapter 10
School and Summer

The following school year, one of the students asked me what I looked like in high school. I said I was skinnier but not much different and why do you care? He said he just wanted to know and was going to look me up on classmates.com.

"Where'd you go to high school?"

"I'm not telling you that. You have to figure it out. I'll give you some clues, though. The town starts with a T and it's in a state that starts with a C," I replied.

"All right, is it Kansas?"

"Kansas? Where'd you learn to spell, and do I even have a remote Southern accent?"

"All right, I'll Google the states."

"There aren't too many so it shouldn't be hard."

"Connecticut?"

"Right, now find the town."

"Trumbull?"

"No, where was John Brown born?"

"Torrington."

"Right."

"I can't find the information I need for classmates. com? Why?"

"I don't know; I never use that stuff."

I continued to get e-mails from classmates.com for two more years. I even went to the technology department to get classmates.com off of my computer but it kept coming back. I started getting e-mails from people that I had gone to school with, and it got irritating.

That year happened to be one of the high school reunion years. Before the five-year reunion, one of my friends, Paul, from high school, called me up, "Are you going? The power is out here, and I'm sitting with my daughter with candles lit."

"Are you all right? You don't sound so good." I was a little concerned because he had been a good friend.

"I'm fine."

"I can't go because I'm on duty that weekend." It was a lie, but I really didn't want to go. I never planned on going back to a reunion. I hadn't seen Paul since his wedding. We were just out of college, and he was already getting married. Then I asked him, "So how's it going?" and the conversation became like a call he would have with his boss, not a long time friend.

He became real serious. "I divorced Christine last year and started dating Jen a couple of months later. We got married that year. She died during childbirth, but my daughter survived. I then moved into a house next to my deceased wife's parents. Christine moved in with me to help with my daughter."

"Do you think that was such a great idea? Don't you think Jen's parents would get mad?"

Then he just dropped the conversation. "I got my master's in economics and now work for the state of Connecticut. I have to go now." It was a very disjointed conversation, but I did remind him to call back after the reunion.

Paul did call back after the reunion and said, "The reunion was great. You should have been there. All of the soccer players sat with the soccer players, and the football players sat with the football players."

"Paul, that sounds pathetic. I would never want to be involved with something like that." I never heard from him again.

Years later, I got an e-mail from Debbie, who had been the class president my senior year. She e-mailed me to inform me of another class reunion. She said she wasn't asking me to do anything for the reunion because she knew I wouldn't do it anyway. That kind of turned me off, but it was true. I had been class treasurer for the four years I was in high school, and I was supposed to help with reunions. I also wasn't fond of Debbie's aunt, who'd been the student council supervisor. She would say to me, almost every week, "Fran, all you do is sit around here and collect dust." She was also right.

I used to spend two hours at lunch because if I didn't have lunch, I had homeroom. My homeroom teacher was Mr. Carroll, who was the speech therapist and who, oddly enough, had a speech impediment. He just wanted the kids out of the room so any excuse we gave him, he accepted. I used to tell him I had a student council meeting, and he would let me go. Then I hung out at lunch. I used to think I was being slick and faking out Mr. Carroll, but now, after teaching for so many years, I realize that he didn't care where I was going; it was just one less kid he had to deal with.

That's the reason I was in clubs—to get out of homeroom. I was in varsity club but only went to the activities I wanted to, like the pro wrestling matches. Those were fun because we would get there early and screw around in the ring. It was almost like a trampoline, and my father was the doctor who had to take the blood pressure of the wrestlers. He used to say that they all had high blood pressure, were taking steroids, and were drinking beer with each other while playing cards before their matches. One of the other clubs was French club. I couldn't stand the teacher, but some of the meetings were fun. I liked the frog legs night and thought it was kind of unique at the time.

I told Debbie I would try to get to that reunion, but I never went.

About halfway through that year, the academic administrator told us that most of the classes were going to be changed because several teachers were either leaving or retiring. I had been teaching tenth-grade for a number of years and enjoyed it. By that time, the kids were mature enough to hold a decent conversation; I didn't want to lose that class. I hoped, instead, that I'd lose the eighth grade class.

I really didn't like those two sections of eighth-grade that year and was sick of it. The parents just wanted the teacher to fix their kid and would complain to the administration if their son was doing poorly. I knew that some of the parents were doing their sons' homework—any time I gave the students something to do in class, it was totally different than if they turned it in after working on it at home.

This was also about the time when the kids really got into the Internet and figured out ways to plagiarize their papers. I had one student who would just print out a paper from the Internet and cut off the name of the person who had done the work. He'd do it right in front of me and didn't seem to care. I'd say, "You know I'm going to flunk you on that paper."

He'd just shrug his shoulders. "So what? I don't care. It's done."

I also had students hand in papers that read, "In this chapter you will learn." They didn't even read the site that they were copying from. Students also would take information from Wikipedia. I used to tell them that Wikipedia was not a reliable source because anyone could log on to the site and change the information.

One incident caused me to lighten up on the whole plagiarism thing. I had caught a number of students and it wasn't hard to do. Especially for someone that woke up so early. The incident involved a local student whose family was also in litigation with another school district. I presume it was over the same kind of thing. I called my father and brothers for advise. All of them said, "Do not call this woman, anything you say can be misconstrued and used against you in court."

I replied, "In court? I don't want to go to court for anything and plagiarism is just a stupid reason and a waist of tax payer's money."

After that, I lightened up on the plagiarism thing. I talked to my father, saying, "I really don't care if they are copying their work. It's no skin off my back, but it isn't worth turning them in, not if I'm going to get sued and possibly lose my job."

"I agree; just let it go."

I was a little ticked off at the process and myself. My ethics seemed to be going down the drain, but any time a kid had a problem, it seemed to be a bigger problem for me with the administration. It irritated the hell out of me. I used to make fun of the older teachers because the kids would tell me what was happening in those classes, and that they got away with all kinds of stuff. I prided myself on not being like those teachers, but things and events were changing. I wasn't able to put an outline of the day's notes on the board each day. I was never told why I couldn't put the outline up but I presume it had something to do with my bad handwriting. I never stopped getting flack for that, from everyone. I had to e-mail the outline to the students. That didn't bother me much because my hands were in such bad shape that it didn't hurt as much. It was easier to type than write because my hands didn't cramp up like they had been. We also had to stop putting our detention list on the board because we were told it was public humiliation. We had to e-mail the detention list to the kids and to whoever happened to be on duty that weekend. I knew that wouldn't work. The kids would say they never got the e-mail and the on duty person didn't care because that was just fewer kids. In seventeen years, I never got any of the assignments that the kids were supposed to complete in detention. The ODs were supposed to write up the kids who didn't show up but they rarely did because that was more work for them. For the most part, the kids knew more about the computer system and firewall at the school than the adults did, so they would override the system or get the system to crash.

I was getting older, and I knew that if I wanted to move on, it would have to be soon. I was dissatisfied with the whole school process and kind of wanted out, but I didn't have enough money to just quit. I didn't want to rely on my father, and I really didn't want to move back home. On one of his visits in 1997, I said, "I'm sick of this shit. The education of the students doesn't seem to be important any more. All the administrators seem to want to do is keep everyone happy, and I don't mean the teachers. They don't want any legal problems or a bad reputation, and this school already has a reputation as a reform school. I want to quit because I don't want to be stuck like the rest of these teachers. They don't make enough money and can't just pick up and leave like I can. All I have is myself. I'm the only one I have to take care of and for the past five years, I've wanted to move to Alaska and tell everyone to get lost. I'm also starting to complain too much, just like everyone else at this school and I can't stand when they do that."

"Take it easy, Fran. I'll be supportive in whatever you do."

It was another ten years before I did anything about my situation and quit.

From there, I just put up with school politics and spent as little money as possible. I liked the summers the best, for obvious reasons, and because I spent less money. I'd travel each summer but it was always on standby. I did what I thought was right, which didn't always work out, and I would continue going into school between 4:00 a.m. and 5:00 a.m. for tutorials.

Since the academic administrator changed the classes halfway through that year, all of the teachers had already submitted their books and materials for the year to come. I was switched from tenth grade history to ninth grade history, which was to include all of world cultures from day one. I thought it would be impossible to get through it all in a year. When I'd taught the tenth grade World Cultures II class, I couldn't get through what I needed to do, and that class was only from 1815 to the present.

"Fran, we have to change tenth grade to American history because a number of kids didn't get into the schools they wanted to because they didn't have a full year of American history. American history is usually taught in the tenth grade."

"I've been teaching tenth grade for ten years, and I would really hate to give it up."

"Sorry, but this is happening to most of the teachers, so you shouldn't feel too bad." Damn, I had to give up everything I've had prepped for in the last ten years because the guidance department messed up and didn't schedule the right classes for the kids.

"Oh, you will also lose the eighth grade and get the advanced-placement class."

That made me a little happier, until my department head said, "Yeah, that was offered to me, but I turned it down because there's too much work involved."

I said to the academic administrator, "I can deal with it, but I need to order new books for the AP class and ninth grade class."

"I'll check into it for you."

A little later in the day, I got an e-mail from him saying that there wasn't enough money in the history budget for me to get new books. I read the e-mail to my tenth-grade class and said, "If he had told us we were switching classes before we ordered books for next year, there would be enough money in the budget." It also meant that I would have the same kids in class next year that I had in eighth-grade this year.

Later on that day, I got an e-mail saying that I had to complete the course syllabus for my new classes by next week, and I should forward my course outline to the teacher who would be teaching my old classes. I figured I would just copy the outlines from the other teachers who taught the courses that I was going to teach. I sure as hell didn't want to do it again. The first time we had to create a course outline, we were told that we wouldn't get paid until we finished it. Kyle Grange and I worked on it all weekend and finished ours. My outlines were about twenty-two pages each.

Herb Frost, another teacher, never did his because he knew he was retiring, and the AP teacher knew he was leaving, too, so he never did his. I locked myself in the house that weekend and pounded out the advanced-placement syllabus, and then I started to think about it.

"This guy's a math teacher, and he has already said he doesn't know anything about history," I told myself, "Shit, I'll just send him the same stuff and change the class title. He won't know because the new teacher has to set up a new syllabus for the American history class. This has to work. I know it's all just paperwork and nobody is looking through it. It's all to satisfy Middle States and they probably aren't looking through it either. I know people that have done Middle States, and a lot of them aren't the most reliable people in the first place. The purpose was to inundate them with paperwork until they were overwhelmed, and then they just give up and say it's fine."

This stuff happened all the time. Kids did it all the time. I know specific teachers who never read the homework, and the kids would actually do the work on the first page, and then on the second page, they'd write, "I know you're not reading this," over and over again.

I received an e-mail from the academic administrator the following day that informed me that I had to go to a training session for new AP teachers. He said that he would leave the information in my mailbox and that I should start working on it as soon as possible so I could get registered. After reading the information, I asked the academic administrator, "Will I be taking the class for credit or will I be auditing it?"

"You'll be auditing it because it cost less. You also will be staying at the Super 8 Motel instead of the Ramada Inn, like the others, because it's cheaper."

I didn't care about the motel because I didn't want to associate with the other teachers anyway—I'm not much of a talker—but I wanted credit for taking the classes. I talked to the English AP teacher who had to go up to Watertown, Connecticut, for her conference. I told her, "The place is nice, once you get out of the train terminal in Waterbury. My father grew up there, but it has become semi-dangerous over the years. You'll probably have to get a taxi to Watertown, and if you are anywhere around Taft, there is no where to stay."

She said, "I like conferences but you're going to have a tough time because you don't talk enough."

"Great, and I get to go to Wilkes-Barre, Pennsylvania."

At the end of that year there was a retirement party for my department head at the headmaster's house. I'm not big on those parties, but this guy had been really good to me, so I went. I always felt uncomfortable at those parties, and in the seventeen years that I taught at the school, I only went to four social functions. At the first one, I hung out in the kitchen with the staff, snuck out the back door, and walked home. At the second and third one, a number of us had a few beers, and I actually had a good time. I went to the last one only to see how my raise, which we never got, was being spent on the headmaster's new house.

At that retirement party, I ran into the academic administrator when I was getting food, and he said, "So Fran, how are you spending your summer? I like to live vicariously through my co-workers."

"Well, since you changed all of my classes and I have no books, I guess I'll be preparing my new classes. Then I get to go to an AP seminar in the middle of the summer."

He rolled his eyes and said, "Okay."

I was surprised by my response but was happy with the outcome.

That summer I was kind of worried about the seminar. I'm never good at that kind of thing, so I tried to prepare and found out that there would be 180 people there. I thought, *Great I can get lost in the crowd and not have to go to all the seminars*. I had called ahead a number of times to find out what I needed to do. I also got a map to find a better route to Wilkes-Barre because I hated the tunnels on the Northeast Extension. I found a route up Route 100 and followed it. Finally, I had to look at the map again, but I couldn't find the road. Then a woman came out of the house across the street from where I'd stopped and asked if I was lost.

"No, I don't think so. There's nothing around here that is on the map, though."

"Oh, that map is wrong. That road was never finished, and the only way to get there is up the Northeast Extension."

"Thanks," I said, and I turned around to get my stuff together for the next day.

The next day I left early so I could get there before everyone else, pick up my packets, and really find out what was going on. When I got there, there was no place to park; it didn't even look like a college. It was a bunch of old houses that turned out to be classrooms. I finally asked, "Could you tell me where Wilkes University is? I've been looking for over an hour."

"You're in it."

"But there isn't any place to park?"

"You can park in my driveway," she replied.

I thought, *Wow, what a nice lady and she doesn't even know me.*

I was there before everyone else, even before the staff had set up the information. I helped so I could get my material faster. While I was there, this old guy showed up, sweating worse than me, and asked for his packet. It turned out he was in the history section also, so I asked, "Are you taking the course?"

"No, I'm the professor."

"How many people are in the class?" I asked, expecting 180.

"Only five."

"I thought there would be 180?"

"No, that's for the entire seminar. Here's our list."

Man, this was going to stink. "How many are taking the class for credit and how many are auditing?"

"That doesn't matter because everyone is going to do the same thing. I know that the auditors don't have to do the computer work that the credit people do, but they'll be doing it."

"Oh, I didn't know that there was computer work involved."

"Yes, we'll be doing that for a few days."

I hadn't planned to do any drinking, but in the matter of a couple hours, I reneged on my no-drinking policy. I got to my room and tried to get ice out of the machine but it was broken. I tried the other floors, but the ice machines were all broken. I thought the night couldn't get much worse but it did; the beer was skunked. I choked one down anyway.

The next day I got to Wilkes University early to get a decent seat, but I couldn't find the correct house/ classroom. I almost called it quits, but then I finally found it. I sat down with a few other people and thought, *Wow, these people look kind of young.* It turned out that two other people and I were in the wrong classroom. Ours was across the hall. The first thing I did was turn down the thermostat to sixty-five degrees. It was the middle of July and really hot. Only one other person showed up, plus the professor. Supposedly, one guy was sick. That would have been a good excuse to make but I really don't think it would have worked for me since I'm such a terrible lier. The professor asked each of us about our background and teaching philosophy. I really didn't have a teaching philosophy. I did what I thought was right and what would benefit the students, but I made some things up and talked about the number of foreigners in the school. That worked at first, but after an hour or so, the professor said, "Mr. Finn, you've been really quiet lately." By that time, I had realized that these people were way more into teaching AP than I was, or they could lie better than I could. It didn't matter; I was kind of turned off by them and was really glad we weren't in the same hotel. I had thoughts of them coming over at night to study; that wasn't going to happen. At about 10:00 a.m., it was break time. I wanted to go out and have a chew, but the professor said, "Why don't we all go to break together?"

Damn, this guy was starting to get on my nerves. I got something to drink while the others continued to talk about teaching. Shit, teaching was something I did to make a living, but I didn't live it. So I went into the bathroom and put in a nice healthy chew.

After break we continued with the class and were given a number of books that the professor used to teach his class. I grabbed as many as I could because I knew there wasn't money in the budget for more of these books. I got a couple of strange looks, but I just put them on the chair next to me and ignored the other people. At noon, the professor said, "Let's all go to lunch together."

I said, "I'm sorry, but my school didn't include lunch in my package."

Actually, the school had offered, but I knew I wouldn't like hanging out with these people, so I deferred. That was one of the right decisions that I made. So I grabbed all my books and went to a Chinese restaurant as I tried to figure out what I was going to do. This seminar was supposed to be five days long, and I didn't think I could manage that. I'd only been there four hours, and these people were already really bothering me. Why couldn't I go to a one-day seminar, like Carol did for the AP English class?

While I was eating my food I thought, *Screw this. This school is so unorganized that they won't even know if I was at the seminar.* My father used to tell me about the medical seminars that people went to—they would collect the information and then go and play golf the rest of the time. I had the books and the professor's syllabus. I didn't need that other stuff. I'd just copy his syllabus and tweak it to what I needed.

So I went back to the hotel and blew off the rest of the seminar. The problem was that I had to waste four more days, and there really wasn't anything to do in Wilkes-Barre. I was pretty bored by the second day, but I knew that if I checked out, the school would know that I left early because they would be billed. I figured that I could make up some excuse, and so I checked out the next day.

When I got home my neighbor, who I taught with, yelled, "I knew you wouldn't make it." I told him about it and that my excuse was that my sister was moving and needed my truck. She *was* moving, but I never helped her move. What shocked me a bit was that I got a call from the director of the seminar. I wasn't prepared for that and stumbled through my excuse. She said that because I hadn't finished the seminar, I wouldn't be certified to teach AP history. I thought I was in trouble then. The academic administrator was bound to pick up on that, and this seminar cost over a thousand dollars. Then I got a call from the business department saying that they got a bill from the Super 8 that indicated that I'd checked out three days early. I told the woman in the business department that the Super 8 was too close to the highway, so I'd found another motel and paid for it myself. I never heard another word about any of it.

Chapter 11
AP, Teachers Residuals and Sensitivity

My first year of teaching advanced-placement was in 2000. I had a good group of kids, only six, but I had no idea on what I was doing, and I know the seminar wouldn't have helped anyway. I hadn't stolen enough books, so I had to make copies of the books I did have. I told one kid, Trevor, "You should never take a class that is offered by a first-year teacher of that class."

"Why not?"

"Because the new teacher pretty much doesn't know anything about the subject yet." I then told him about Father Willis.

I had been told that Father Willis' class, Ethics, was an easy "A," and that I should take his class. It might have been easy at one time, but by the time I took it during my senior year, the class was tough. I wasn't doing well, but I did know Father Willis well. I asked him, "Why is this class so hard? It's only an elective and my girlfriend, Tammy, told me it was easy. That's the only reason I took it. No offense."

"When Tammy took it, it was my first year teaching it," Father Willis explained, "and I had no idea of what I was doing. Now I do."

At the end of the year, he asked me what I wanted for a grade.

"I want an A," I told him.

"I can't give you an A, but I'll give you a B," which kind of negated the title of the class.

Good relationships with your teachers always pays off.

That first year, I had no idea what was going on. I set up my syllabus and summer reading. The summer reading was to be *Mein Kampf*. I had to read *Mein Kampf* in graduate school and figured I would mess with the kid's heads. I couldn't even get through *Mein Kampf* in grad school. Hitler was one messed-up guy. I didn't know at that point, but what I was supposed to be teaching was AP United States history. No one had told me. I had taken AP history and English in high school, but the history part was world history. I didn't know it was AP United States history until a kid, who had taken the course the year before, said to me on the senior trip, "Why did you have them read *Mein Kampf*? It's a United States history class."

Well, the AP class did really poorly that year on the AP exam. I had the kids do three three-page essays a week on certain topics and told them to review all the material that we had covered that year before the exam.

A number of the kids, however, were taking as many AP classes as possible, and the history AP test was the last one on the day before the SATs. The kids had to pay for the AP test themselves, and it was taken unconventionally. Usually, when kids take the AP exam, it's at a central location, like a local high school, where everyone from the surrounding area takes it together. That wasn't the case here. These exams were taken on the third-floor of the main building, and a cottage faculty administered the exam. The students were allowed to eat and go to the bathroom whenever they wanted. I even heard that the guy who taught the class before me had all the answers and gave them to the kids.

At the usual AP exams, there might be a person from the state who made sure that the rules, which are strictly laid out, were followed. Each area of the exam was examined and timed. If the time for the directions was up, it was up, and then you had to proceed.

That wasn't the case at this school; things happened as things happened. If someone from the AP organization came in, the cottage faculty was called by the academic administrator, and the kids were instructed to throw away any food or drink they had and to be quiet.

To get college credit for the AP course a person had to get a four or a five on the test. The scale is from one to five, and some schools accepted a three. I used to tell the kids that most of the questions wouldn't be about the world wars or about other major conflicts. I showed them percentage charts of questions in the front of the book and said they had to be well versed in each section. I said, "Yes, the major points in history are the most fun to learn, but that's not what they are going to ask you, most likely. They are going to ask you strange things like, 'What was the first major league baseball team?' or 'Where are the Seminoles from?'"

The foreign students hated these questions. They could memorize anything, but they really didn't know what it meant. I used to try to give them hints about the questions like, "What is Florida State's football team named? What is the name of the Pittsburgh football team and why are they called that, and why are the New York Knicks called the New York Knicks?" Most of the students couldn't get them and did terrible on the exam.

The foreign students used to say, "I don't care about American football or basketball."

"Guys, that doesn't matter; these are hints. The Florida State team is called the Seminoles because the Seminoles were from Florida; the Steelers are called the Steelers because of the influx of steel in western Pennsylvania; and the Knicks were named after the Dutch settlers, who were called Knickerbockers." It just didn't seem to work. That didn't mean anything to foreigners who, ironically, were the majority of my classes over the past seven years. Last year, the two American students I had dropped out because of the amount of work.

I also had a government class. I didn't really like the class and, oddly enough, as a former history teacher, I could not care less about the government. I would have those students write three two-page papers a week on related subjects. The kids hated them, but they seemed to like me and hated the other teachers that were offering electives. One student, Charles, said, "These papers suck, but at least we know what we're getting with you. You give us a syllabus of all the essays we'll have to write for the semester, so we can work ahead. The other teachers seem to wake up and say, 'Okay, what am I going to do today?'" I kind of appreciated that, and I liked Charles and the other students in the class. We had fun and talked about current events.

One student, Joe, asked me if I had to write papers in high school like those I assigned to them. I told him, "I didn't; when I was in high school I might have written three, but when I got to college I had an American Documents class, and I had a five-page paper due every Friday. It was my freshman year, and I couldn't handle it. I'm not proud to say it, but I flunked the class and had to take a summer course in art history. You think this is boring; take art history. If you learn this stuff now, like I should have, you should do fine. Contrary to what you think and have told me, I hate correcting these papers. It takes hours, and it is really boring."

Last year, Joe came back for a visit, and he told me that it did help since he really learned how to do research.

A number of teachers weren't qualified to teach classes. Having been a substitute teacher when I was younger, I knew that the law dictated that someone had to have at least two years of college before he or she could sub. Many of the cottage faculty that substituted didn't have college degrees. Even some of the regular teachers didn't have a degree—or they didn't have degrees in what they taught. For example, one teachers had a degree in physical education, but since he was from Puerto Rico and spoke Spanish, he taught it for over ten years. Another Spanish teacher had a master's in math but taught Spanish, also because he was from Puerto Rico. The former English teacher had a degree in French and after she left, the academic administrator asked me to teach beginning French because I had taken French in high school. I said, "I can't do that. I was never really good at French."

"How about World Religions?" the administrator asked. "Your name is Finn, so you have to be Catholic."

"Yeah, I know, but I'm as close to being agnostic as could be accepted by my family."

"That doesn't matter; just do it," the administrator said.

The department head for English has a degree in public speaking. The assistant headmaster has a degree in shop. The headmaster had a degree in finance. The current academic administrator has a master's in humanities. At least I had a degree in history and was teaching history. When the classes were changed around, and I got ninth grade and AP, one of the Korean students, Suk Won, asked his guidance counselor if he could get me for his independent study teacher for his AP Modern European history class. That AP class wasn't offered at the school, but he wanted the credits. The counselor told him that my background was in American history. Suk Won then came to my classroom and said, "My guidance counselor said I couldn't take you because your background is in American history."

"Suk Won, she doesn't know what she's talking about. She doesn't know what I went to school for. She started working here about eight years after I started. Man, I went to school for European history, and all she's looking at is what I've taught since I've been here. She has no idea what I know." I continued to explain, "When someone starts working here, they just pick up the classes of the person they're replacing. That's why I have the classes I have. It doesn't matter how much a person knows about the material or if he likes it; that's what he gets, and that is that."

I did do independent study a number of years ago with a senior who wouldn't have graduated unless I did it. Mark was a decent kid, so I agreed. I had been warned by another teacher about picking up extra classes because, he told me, the school is shady. He told me that he had been offered about three thousand dollars more if he picked up an extra class. He agreed but, as was usual at this school, everything was an oral agreement. At the end of the year, he asked why he hadn't gotten paid, and the school administrators said they didn't know what he was talking about. I knew this would happen, so I pretty much just gave Mark things to do, and I wasn't there most of the time.

I used to say that every one of the teachers would get fired in a minute if they were working at a different school. As teachers, we got away with so much. Every once in a while, the kids would ask, "Why do you stay here and put up with this crap from the administration? You don't even seem to enjoy it."

"It would be tough to work at another school, since my identity is pretty much engrained here," I replied.

"What's that mean?"

"It means that if I hit a kid, he knows I am kidding, and it won't be a problem. If I did that anywhere else, I'd be fired and arrested. If I hit you, you can hit me back. If I say something disrespectful on purpose or by mistake, you can do the same to me. It sounds weird, but I want an open relationship, and you guys know that. That doesn't work in other places."

Obviously this didn't always work, and eventually, I got in trouble with the administration. Many times I would hear teachers yell at the kids to shut up. I did it a number of times myself. It was amazing what we got away with. The headmaster caught me pushing a kid against the wall. The headmaster just shrugged it off like it was no big deal.

One of the other history teachers told me that he broke a kid's arm when showing him a wrestling move, and all he got as a result was a slap on the wrist from the administration. An old English teacher hung a kid out the second-floor window of his classroom. The art teacher saw this and ran like a linebacker down the hallway. She was knocking the hell out of the kids in the hallway to get to the classroom. That teacher did almost get fired for that one.

One former Spanish teacher yelled at a kid, and as the kid walked away, the teacher threw the Spanish text book at him, hitting the kid in the back of the head. Nothing happened. The place was starting to get out of control. The former German teacher used to throw his keys and other objects at the kids if he thought they weren't listening. Another history teacher has tennis balls that he throws at the kids if they aren't listening. There have been teachers that have hit kids with chairs and punched kids in the face. Any one of us could have been fired at any time.

I did get in trouble in 2005 for calling a kid a fag during assembly. The kid was sitting right behind me and said something derogatory to me. I just turned around and said, "Shut up faggot." Somehow, a homosexual teacher heard me. Later on that day, he came to my room and said, "Fran, I don't appreciate you saying that word. Personally, I am offended."

I explained to the teacher that I hadn't meant anything by it. I said, "When I was in high school in the mid-1980s, my coach would call us Commie Pinko Fags if we didn't do something he wanted us to do. I know it had a total different meaning because of the Cold War, but it never was a big deal. My father would even call us fags if he thought we weren't trying hard enough. Really, I was only kidding."

"Fran, it has a total different connotation now than when you were growing up, and the term shouldn't be used."

I reluctantly agreed and thought, *Mother fucker, you're not that much younger than I am; don't be so sensitive.*

When did everyone get so sensitive? I grew up in New England and went to college in New England. I guess people up north are a little more tough-skinned. I can't handle sensitive people. My family is not sensitive, so I never grew up that way. If you did something and someone didn't like it, that person would say, "Shit head, cut it out."

That has always been the way in my family. My mother never cursed, but when she wasn't around, it was almost like free game on any one of us. If we even said anything remotely abusive in front of my mother, it cost us one way or another. It might be early bed or more work around the house, and if we said shut up to anyone and my mother heard us, it cost us a quarter. In my family, that added up. Each night, one of us had to do the dishes. It got to the point where whoever was on dish duty didn't eat because everyone else used as many dishes as possible to make it more difficult on the dishwasher.

We kids did find ways to antagonize each other. My brother Pat was the worst and the best at it. He used to put stuff in our beds all the time, like putty, weights so we banged our knees when we jumped in bed, and some substance that looked like snot. If we were in the kitchen and no one else was around besides my brothers, we knew we'd end up in the trash can. Mike was older, so he would just punch us. Ginny used to blow her nose in the sheets, or she would try to get me to get sick. She knew what I didn't like, and it didn't matter what it was—she would get it to drive me nuts. For instance, I had a weird hatred for lint. It used to make me gag, and I don't know why. Any time Ginny found lint, she would come to find me and chase me. She knew it would set me off, and it always did.

Ginny was the best athlete in the family, and I could never get away from her or catch her. The strange thing is that today, I'm closer to Ginny than anyone else in my family. My sister Sheila just told us all to get lost and did her own thing. We all tried to get back at each other. Mike never really had to get back at any of us because he could beat the hell out of all of us. Pat was a little different. When Ginny was really young, he shaved her head, and when I was about six, I pushed him off the top bunk of the bed. Pat was really into animals and reptiles so I took two of Pat's small turtles and fried them in the toaster. There was always a way to get back at each other. Somehow, Sheila seemed to come away unscathed.

Because my father is a doctor and my mother was a school nurse, dinner conversations were not conventional.

We talked about vaginal warts, lung cancer, and other various diseases, and there was no holding back on the details. We were just used to it. Once, a woman I was dating came over for dinner, and we all were talking about boils on someone's genitals. She excused herself and threw up the veal in the toilet.

The most recent incident was after I got hit in the back of the head, working at a distribution company. I had to get stitches and was thinking about a lawsuit. I didn't want to do it because I didn't want to go to court, and I hate people who sue for stupid things, but I figured I would look into it anyway. The thing that bothered me was that I was treated like a leper by the other workers and no one would help me because, apparently, everyone is afraid of AIDS. I wanted to say, "I don't do drugs and I haven't been laid in a long time. If I had AIDS, I'd be dead by now." The floor manager just told me to clean off the back of my head and go back to work, which I did, until I got dizzy.

I continued to bleed and soaked the upper part of my shirt as I drove home. By this time, I had resigned from the school and was living at a friend's house. It was about 5:00 a.m. when he got up for work and saw my head. He said, "Jesus Christ, I think I'm going to throw up. Are you all right?"

"I can't really think straight," I said. I had a paper towel pressed to the back of my head.

"You shouldn't be drinking beer; it'll thin your blood and you won't clot."

"I know, and I don't care. This might be 5:00 a.m. to you but I work third shift. This is about 5:00 p.m. for me."

The problem was that I didn't have any health insurance. I lost that when I left teaching. I had never used it in the seventeen years I worked there, so after leaving the school, I didn't even worry about it. I figured nothing would happen. It was stupid; in the next two weeks, I would go to the walk-in medical center three times.

We should have taken pictures, but Ben was focused on trying to stop the bleeding. Then he called school and told them that I had had an accident and he had to drive me to the walk-in center because I was unfit to drive. I've had concussions before, and I knew the worst thing possible was to go to sleep. Still, after Ben stopped the bleeding, I went to bed. He gave me a hat so I wouldn't bleed in the bed, and then said he was going shopping and to the movies. He had used my injury as an excuse for a day off.

Ben got back hours later, and I was still in bed. He came in to see how I was and told me to get up and put some clothes on. "Your head is swollen. I'm taking you to the walk-in center."

"I have to shower first because I look like shit."

"No, the worse you look the better it will be." We went back to the distributor, and I said I wanted the injury report. I also said I wouldn't be working there any more; that I didn't need brain damage; and that I would be back in a day or so with my paperwork.

When we got to the walk-in center, Ben filled out the paperwork for me because I was a little shaky. He asked me, "So have you had any previous injuries?"

"I've fractured my scull and broken six ribs, an arm, a leg, my hip, and my hands and fingers a number of times.

I fell out of a car once and had to spend two weeks inside so the side of my face could heal."

"Shit, Fran, you're a mess, and there's no more room left to write."

Then we waited for the doctor. After a couple of hours, it was my turn, and I went in for a tetanus shot and got my blood pressure taken. The doctor then cleaned out my wound—Ben had filled it with a couple of septic sticks to stop the bleeding—and stitched me up. She asked, "Do you take aspirin every day because there is a lot of blood? If not, are you a smoker?"

"No, I'm not a smoker but I do chew tobacco."

She gave me a dirty look, and said, "Don't get your head wet for a few days, and come back in two days for a checkup."

Out of curiosity I asked, "When can I go back to work?"

"Tomorrow, but don't get hit in the head again."

Later on, I found out that many distributor places kind of have a deal with the walk-in centers. Most of these people that work third shift don't have medical insurance, and it benefits both the company and the center if the person goes back to work right away—both places continue to make money.

A couple days later I went back for my checkup, and the doctor was surprised by the size of my head. "Your head shrank and the stitches are loose. Remember, keep your head dry." She said I could get my stitches out in seven to ten days.

I kind of had a sick pleasure about getting stitches out; it felt good to me. I've had plenty of stitches in my life, and it's always been pleasurable for me to have the stitches removed. After this incident, though, I did want some advice.

So I called Mike, who is a workmen's compensation lawyer; he deals with this thing all the time. I explained my situation, and he told me that Congress had passed laws in the 1920s and 1930s about lawsuits against distributors, and that I couldn't win; it wasn't worth trying. Everyone I had talked to previously had said that I would win a lawsuit because of negligence and that they allowed me to drive myself home, knowing I was injured.

Mike was a little short and obviously preoccupied with something, so I called my father, who suggested that I call my other brother, Pat. I didn't call Pat right away because I knew I'd be seeing him in a couple weeks.

When my father, Mike, Pat, and Carol went over to my sister Ginny's about a month after my accident, Mike was the first to ask about it. "Can I see the scar," he asked, as he poked at my head? "Did you make a claim yet? You know, you have a year to do it."

"Mike, you told me in our last conversation that I couldn't sue because the corporations were covered."

"No, you still can. Don't you listen?"

"Mike, do you remember the last thing you said to me when we saw each other at your house?"

"No"

"You said, 'Fran, I've only got one thing to say to you: get your teeth fixed.'" He just looked at me after that and asked to see my truck. On the night that I was at his house, I slept there until 3:00 a.m., pissed off the back of his porch, and drove the five hours home. That's how sensitive we are.

Chapter 12
Iceland

That summer I decided to finally go somewhere where I was comfortably cold. All the other places I'd been were too loud and hot. John wanted to go to Vietnam, which I always wanted to visit, but at the time, there was no United States embassy, and I thought it was kind of a risk. Then we talked to another teacher and decided it wasn't a good option. He said, "It's really hot, and you have to hire a driver or go on a tour, as it is impossible to drive there."

Then John told him, "Fran gets up early and walks around wherever we are."

"He better not do that in Vietnam before the sun comes up, or he'll probably be killed." That crossed Vietnam off my list for the time being. I didn't like the heat, but getting killed could happen anywhere.

The first place I thought of was Greenland. I wanted to go to the top of the earth and had the resources to do it. John went out and bought a bunch of books and added them to the collection he already had. We split them up and read through them. Greenland is huge, but there aren't many roads, and everything is imported. I already knew the history of Greenland to some extent—that the Vikings called it Greenland because when they were pillaging in Iceland, they named the areas. They didn't want people to go to Iceland, so they named the two areas, hoping people would go to Greenland, as the name seemed more appealing than Iceland.

We learned that Greenland was really expensive, so we settled on Iceland, which turned out to be an excellent choice, even though it was also expensive as hell.

I drove up to John's house and we left for Logan Airport a few days later by train.

Once got there we had to rush to get to the next terminal. Logan Airport is huge, and after John drinks his sodas each morning, he gets all hyped up. I had a tough time keeping up and was sweating a lot. It was about ninety degrees, and I was in shorts and a T-shirt. I had packed my work boots in my duffle bag and was wearing loafers—it's a wimpy look but airport compatible. Everything always seems to be hurry-up-and-wait; I hate that. Once at the airport, we sat for another two hours. I mellowed out at the bar but continued to get greasier. Finally, our flight was there. There was only one seat left in standby, but luckily, someone didn't show up for the flight, and we both got on. By that time it was getting late, and we ran into a really drunk Icelandic guy. He slapped me on the chest and said, laughing, "It's not summer in

Iceland. Drink up now, because you'll be paying for it later."

We had read the books, and I always look for whether or not the location has chew and how much it costs. I also look for the price of beer. I found neither when I researched Iceland. I never take a chance with the Copenhagen thing and make sure I have enough stored away for the trip. Beer had never been an issue. Then John looked at me and said, "Wow, we might be in trouble."

On the flight, the only open seats were in first class. I had never flown first class and thought it would be great. It was nicer than coach, but it didn't really seem worth the money. I had more leg room and a wider seat, but I still couldn't sleep. About six hours later, we landed in Reykjavik, and the first thing we planned to do was to find a place to stay, but one of the flight attendants said, "Go to the duty-free shop before you leave, after you collect your luggage."

"Why?"

"Oh, you'll find out."

In the duty-free shop, we checked out the prices, which were very expensive. We were only allowed to spend a certain amount, and a twelve-pack of the cheapest beer was twenty-five dollars. We ran into a guy who advised us, "Buy liquor; it's financially more sound."

"John, I hate liquor, but since it's your birthday, we'll buy as much as possible."

From there, we tried to find a place to stay the night, after we got our car. John and I always had a set plan to split everything 50/50—gas, food, or a place to stay. We had planned on camping the entire time, but on the first night, since we were getting older, we like to get a safe place to stay to get our plans together. We drove around the city, looking for the cheapest place, but there weren't any cheap places. We went to close to twelve places, and the prices ranged from $250 to $400 a night. We both had plenty of money, but that was out of line with what we planned on spending.

The first hostel was in Reykjavik, and we learned that the guy in Boston was right—it must have been forty degrees, and I was freezing. I changed my clothes in the car when we stopped at the first hostel, but there were no rooms available. We went to another hostel, but we would have had to share a room with six other people, and we didn't want to do that. We finally ended up close to the lava field by the airport, at another hostel, for about fifty dollars. It was small, and we had to share a bathroom, but at least we got our own room. The first thing John did was go to the community kitchen and get food; I think he might have stolen it.

He told me, "It's fine. Travelers always leave food when they're leaving a hostel. They either are backpacking and don't want to carry it, or they are leaving the country and can't bring it with them."

I thought, *Yeah, but I think they meant that you cook everything here and leave the left overs here. Not take everything and walk away.*

We usually buy and cook our own food, but at the time, I didn't care where John got the food; I was hungry, and everything else was too expensive.

It was summer solstice, so it was light all night. John drank too much and went to bed. I walked around the hostel for a while, but there was no reason to go outside, as I usually did, because we were outside the capital, and there was nothing there. I also didn't want to worry about being locked out of the hostel. All the hostels I've been to have curfews, and they lock their doors. Since I didn't have a watch, I didn't want to risk it. I had forgotten my traveling watch at home, and it drove me absolutely nuts. I can't stand not knowing what time it is. If I wake up at 2:00 a.m., I know I have to stay in bed until at least 4:00 a.m. to be functional the next day, but here it was light twenty-four hours a day. I should have been better prepared, because I made the same mistake in Alaska. I sure as hell wasn't going to buy a watch in Iceland.

That night, I took a bath, which I normally hold off for a while, if not indefinitely. Sometime during the night, John got up, and I really thought he was going to throw up on me because our beds were so close. He ran to the trash can and vomited. After that he said, "Wow, that felt better coming up than going down," and he went back to bed. The next day, we cleaned up the room and the trash can and left before anyone else was up. We were good at that and usually did it, especially if we had messed something up.

I had been in the habit of keeping a log of where and what we did on our trips, but on this trip, I gave up on it. John kept a map and wrote down the mileage, as well as where we were and all the other information that he thought was pertinent. (He now has it hanging in his bathroom, along with a bunch of other pictures of places he's been to).

I was spending a lot of money and decided that since I saw my teaching career coming to an end I'd make the best of my situation and just try to have fun. Ideally, it would have been smart to keep the information of this trip for future use, but I was at the "Fuck it" point.

We had no definitive road plan but hoped on driving pretty much every paved road in Iceland, although there weren't many. It was almost impossible to get into the interior of Iceland because for one, there were no official roads, and two, most of it was desolate. All the areas that were accessible by car were on the coast of the country. So the next day we just started driving. We just picked a road, listened to an Icelandic woman on the travel advice CD, and followed whatever route she gave us. Honestly, the country is the cleanest place I've ever seen. That first day, we stopped at a gas station so I could use the restroom. "John, you have to see this."

"No, I don't. I've seen your shit and I'm not impressed."

"That's not what I mean, it's the cleanest bathroom I've ever seen—and we had a cleaning lady when I was growing up."

John checked it out and agreed, "Wow, it is clean."

"Yeah, in the United States, you really have to be desperate to go to the bathroom at a gas station. I'd rather go in the woods."

Every day, we saw waterfalls and great scenery. We snuck into the Blue Lagoon, which is a geothermal spa that is part of a lava formation and the people there were eating cereal and drinking beer. That's a weird combination, even for us. The place was perfect, and I wanted to move there right away—until I started paying for stuff. Damn, I couldn't afford it; my father and brothers couldn't afford it. A hotdog was a little over five dollars a piece, but they were really good. I only had a few of them because of the price, but I could put anything I wanted on them. The few I had were usually wrapped in bacon, but I could even put cole slaw on them. A soda was another five dollars, so I didn't drink much soda. The one hamburger I got cost ten dollars, and it was really bad. From then on, we just cooked our own food or split a loaf of bread. It was always something simple and affordable.

The biggest deal to us was the cost of beer. We always wanted to be well prepared for the situation we were in. As we got into the first town where we were going to spend the night, we found the beer store—there's not really another name for it. It wasn't a liquor store, like in Connecticut or a beer distributor in Pennsylvania. It was just a beer store. We asked, "What are the hours that this place is open?"

"Usually, we are only open one or two hours a day, in the afternoon. Other towns may have different hours."

"This looks grim, Fran."

"Well, we will have to prepare for every day." We grabbed two cases for $150. "John, I'm going to go broke if this is what it costs."

We paid it and realized that we would have to be a hell of a lot more diligent in our spending if this was the norm. I knew that everything in Iceland was imported, but $75 a case? Man, we were in trouble. Every time we went into a beer store, people were amazed by the amount we spent, but we never knew when it would be open.

That night, we decided to camp. It would save money, and that was our plan anyway. It didn't seem to get very cold at night, even though we didn't know what was usual, having been there only one night, and we'd spent that night inside. We had a tent, and I had brought my summer sleeping bag. I figured it would be fine. That day it was in the sixties and sunny. We had picked a nice site and set everything up. We also went over to the gas station to buy gloves, just in case it got cold. They were crummy gloves, but in a pinch, they would work—at least we hoped they would. We also bought some bread for dinner. We hung out for a while and talked to a couple in a small trailer about the weather and the price of things. The people that we met were extremely nice, except for the owner of the campground. He said, "You two won't make the night."

As we left, I turned to John. "That guy's a real jerk," but as it turned out, in my case he was right.

John went to bed before me, and I just hung out in the midnight sun. Then I spilled water all over my pants. Things went downhill from there. I hadn't brought any other pants. I had packed light, and all I had was a pair of shorts and long johns. Damn, I had planned on sleeping with everything on, even my work boots. I talked to the owner of the campground, and he told me what it would cost to use the washer and dryer. I wasn't really sure how much he was asking, because it wasn't in U.S. currency, but I had to pay for it or I would freeze. After an hour or so, my stuff was dry, and I went to bed. I climbed into the tent with John—he could sleep through almost anything. I learned later that my snoring wasn't one of them. I hadn't brought a pad for under my sleeping bag because I didn't think it would be that cold. I was so off.

That night, I learned that John was used to sleeping against the wall on the floor of his room with his dog. He kept nudging me, like I was the wall, and then pushing me, like I was the dog. John has put up with plenty of my personal quirks, so I really wasn't that mad—but I was really cold. I went to sit in the car but it was cold there, too. I ended up spending the night in the heated bathroom. I had no one to blame but myself. The next day I said, "John, I have to buy a good sleeping bag and a pad. If I don't, I'm going to freeze or spend my nights in the bathroom."

"You're going to pay a hell of a lot for it."

"I know but I have to. Now let's get some hotdogs."

After finding a camping store, John said, "Fran, I found a sleeping bag that goes down to minus fifty degrees. It's going to set you back a bit because it's eighty dollars."

"That's fine. I found a pad for twenty dollars."

The pad and sleeping bag weren't as expensive as I thought they would be. It didn't really matter how much they cost, though, because I knew we would be camping the rest of the trip, and I might not last if I continued like the night before. I figured that if I kept my clothes on, that would be fine.

The next day we drove along the coast again and found a great area. It was right by the penis museum in Húsavik. I don't know why someone would have a penis museum or why the penises of different mammals needed to be displayed, but we stopped in front of the museum, and John asked, "Do you want to go in?"

"Why the hell would I want to do that?"

"Good, I don't want to, either."

That night we found a campground in the middle of town. It started to rain, so we sat in the car for a while, until we went to bed. That night, John kicked me and said, "Quit snoring. You're driving me nuts, and I can't sleep."

I laughed, "Shit, I can't do anything about that."

"You could have gotten those nose strips like I asked you to," he said.

In the morning, I found him sleeping in the trunk of the car. He slept there for the rest of the trip.

The next day we were off again and ran into the columnar basalt formations, which are like the Giant Causeway in Northern Ireland. John climbed on them, until there were too many people around. Then we hit Seljalandsfoss, which has the highest waterfall in Iceland. John took pictures, and I walked around. It was a cool waterfall; people were walking behind it. John walked behind it, too, but I thought, *I can see it from here. How different can the back of the waterfall be?*

From there we went to another small town to camp. We drank a number of beers, and then John decided, "Let's try this dirt road."

"I don't know, John. It's still raining, and we don't have four-wheel drive."

"So what? Let's try. It's a rental anyway."

We went up a steep hill until I asked to stop. I got out to urinate and realized we were at the top of a ski lift. "Look," I called to John, "the chairs are right there."

We continued up the hill, which turned into a mountain, until it got too rocky to drive.

After that, we walked as far as we could go, looking at the markers and taking pictures. These markers were all over the country, and we followed them all the time. They were a bunch of small rocks piled on top of each other and seemed to set a trail for ancient travelers. We never found out really why they were there. There was also a glacier at the top of the mountain, and John gave me the camera, grabbed a piece of plastic out of the car to sit on, and slid halfway down the glacier. That night I went to bed, and he climbed into the trunk of the car again.

The next day we headed down to Hafnarfjordur, the elf capital of the world. The Icelandic people seemed to be very superstitious. There was one story about a road that caused a lot of accidents. They tried to fix the road, but because it was next to an old elf habitat, the road always caused accidents. I thought that was bull, but it was in all the newspapers. It was down south, and we took a dirt road for hours, while Randy Newman was on the radio. Thank God—I was so sick of hearing Coldplay, I could puke. On the way, I fell asleep, and John parked the car on a hill and got out to take a picture. I don't know what happened, but John suddenly opened the door and said, "Shit, Fran! Are you all right?" I woke up when the car hit a pole—it had rolled down the hill about ten feet.

"Sorry, but I forgot to put on the emergency break," John said.

"That doesn't cut it! I almost rolled off the side of the mountain!"

Later that day, while still on the mountain, we ran into a tin survival shed. It was in the middle of nowhere, and we stopped to take a look. I looked through the window first; then we went in. I was surprised because I had never seen anything like that up close. Inside, there was a log book that we read and signed, and then we looked at the books and the survival food that was left there. The place actually looked comfortable. It had a nice bed, but there was no bathroom. Bathrooms are important to me.

From there, we continued down the dirt road to the other side of the mountain and found the elf place. It was a quaint little town, and we went into a few of the shops. I bought what I thought was a cutting board made out of rock. Later on, I found out it was a cheese board. Damn, unmarried and I now had a cheese board. It was expensive, so I just wrapped it in newspaper and packed it up in my things. If it came down to it, I'd just give it to Ginny.

We camped next to a hill where the elves supposedly originated and spent the $75 for a case of beer. Fires were forbidden so we just ate baked beans out of the can, which became way too common.

The following day, we found a place where I could wash my sleeping bag—after too many beers and beans the night before, I'd thrown up on it. It turned out to be a good campground. There was only one other couple there, and it had an enclosed area with a kitchen. Hot food would be great after days of cold baked beans and bread, so we took the stuff that John had stolen from the hostel and made spaghetti. As we were the only ones in the kitchen and it was raining, we started to look around the kitchen and found that the storage door was unlocked. We didn't really find anything, other than small pillows. I had been using a sweatshirt as my pillow, so I grabbed one. Apparently, the supervisor saw what we were doing and came in to lock up the storage closet. He didn't say anything to us, and I'm pretty sure it had to do with the fact that we were drinking beer and hadn't showered in days. After dinner, I went to the tent and John went to the trunk.

We continued to drive along the coast the next day. This place seemed great, but the problem was that we couldn't find a place to stay. There weren't any campgrounds or hostels. We did finally find one hostel that had a tractor in its driveway, but we were told by the owner, "You guys can't stay here until the septic tank is fixed. That will take about five hours."

"John, what the hell are we going to do for five hours? This place isn't even a town. There are only about three hundred people that live here, and the only thing open that I saw was the grocery store."

"Don't worry about it. Let's go to the grocery store and get some crackers." John also got some kind of yogurt drink. On the way out he said, "Wow, this taste really bad. Try it."

I tried it, and then spit it out. "Yes, this tastes bad, and you spent ten dollars on it."

I also bought some dried cod. It was about a foot long, and the first few bites were good, but it got too salty. I was going to throw it away, but John wanted to keep it to put it in his journal. After a couple of days, he threw it out because it started to stink up all his clothes.

We still had plenty of time to waste and couldn't find any place to hang out. We ended up at the church parking lot, drinking beer, but something was happening that day. It wasn't a Sunday, even though I don't really keep track of the days of the week when I'm traveling. I know when I'm leaving, and that's the only important date I need to know.

A lot of people started to show up in the parking lot, and it didn't seem appropriate for us to be there doing what we were doing, so John asked, "Do you want to go up to the cemetery."

"That's fine with me," I said, and so we drove up the dirt road.

Hanging out in a cemetery might not seem right to some people, but I grew up that way. When I was a kid, one of my best friends was Leon Hall; he lived behind a cemetery. We would climb over the fence and play football next to the graves. In high school, I had a friend named Jack whose father was a curator at a cemetery, and we would sneak in and shoot cans off of the headstone.

Luckily, John and I had enough to sustain ourselves for the night—or at least until we could get into the hostel. We had a good time at the cemetery—we read all the gravestones and watched the grave digger bury someone. He didn't seem to mind that we were watching him do it while we were drinking beer.

I've always had a strange affinity for death. I guess having lived with morticians in my family and being a history teacher kind of helped. I have always liked reading the obituaries and finding out what these people did, how they had died, and where they'd gone to school. I used to steal the next-door neighbor's newspaper in the morning and read this stuff. Then I'd put the paper back in the plastic bag and throw it in their driveway.

That night, John and I finally got into the hostel, which was a really nice place. The owner told us, "The first thing you have to do is take off your shoes."

I mumbled, "I hate that; my sister-in-law makes us do that."

Then she went on about the quiet hours, which wouldn't be a problem for us. As in most hostels, we had to share a bathroom, and for two guys who had been messing around for the past five hours, we made a lot of trips. It was obvious that we were making a spectacle of ourselves. Oddly enough, it didn't bother either of us. John went into the kitchen and stole some food again. This time it consisted of bread, ham, cheese, and mustard. We made our sandwiches and left them on the heater, which turned out to be a mistake. Then an Asian guy came to the door and asked questions about our traveling. He asked, "Can my mother and I travel with you? We don't have a vehicle, and we would stay out of the way."

John quickly said, "I'm sorry, but we don't have enough room." We did, but who wants that? We didn't want to baby-sit.

When we went back in the room, I felt a breeze between my legs and said, "Oh, no, I've been talking to that guy for a half-hour, and my zipper has been down." After looking at it, I realized it was broken. "John, you told me to only bring one pair of jeans, and since we've been screwing around so much, I guess I gained weight. What the hell am I going to do now? All I have is a pair of shorts and long johns. Shit, it's Iceland."

"Don't worry about it. I'll take care of it. Put your shorts on, and I'll sew up your zipper with dental floss."

His solution worked, but the problem with that was that every time I had to urinate, I had to pull down my pants. Then we ate our warm ham sandwiches and went to bed.

John asked me the next morning why I was pulling down my pants to go to the bathroom.

"John, you sewed up my zipper last night." He didn't remember anything. A little later that day, I got fed up with the pants, put on my shorts and wore those for the next ten days. If it got cold, I put on my long johns and then my shorts. I didn't care what it looked like—I didn't know anyone, and I wasn't trying to get into *GQ*.

From there, we headed to where we could see icebergs—a long drive up a dirt road—and we followed the stone markers again. We didn't really know where we were going but we just followed the rocks. There were no people anywhere; we hadn't seen people in hours, and we took notice of that.

Finally, we ended up in a desolate place and went over a hill, where there were a lot of icebergs about fifty yards from us. John started to take pictures, and then he gave the camera to me. He said, "I'm going to run down the hill and climb on one of the icebergs. Take my picture once I'm on."

"No problem." He ran down the hill—and then stripped to his boxers. He swam through the water and climbed onto an iceberg. As I started to take his picture, he fell off. I yelled down, "Sorry! I missed that one! You'll have to do it again."

"You did that on purpose."

I actually hadn't, but it was funny.

After that, we crossed over the river, and on the other side was a huge area with a lot of people. We got out to look around, and a bunch of people went up to John and said, "Weren't you that guy in his underwear on the iceberg over there? We all have pictures of you." We got back in the car. John wasn't really embarrassed; I've seen him do worse, and he didn't care. My being in long johns and shorts probably took the edge off, too. Then we found a place to camp—and John went to the trunk.

The next day was Sunday—I knew that it was because all the beer stores were closed. We shopped around but nothing was open, and we didn't have a place to stay. We finally ran into a woman who told us, "All of the stores are closed today but you can go to the grocery store to buy beer. It'll cost you more, though."

"More than seventy-five dollars?"

"Yes, about ten dollars more, and it will be light beer."

"Fran, let's just get it and find a site."

By that time we had gotten used to having no ice and to leaving the beer outside to chill down. During the summer in Iceland, the sports fields at the schools become campgrounds, so that was where we ended up that day. In the rain, we set up the tent, then sat in the car having a beer. After the first one, I said to John, "I think this stuff is skunked. I can't drink it; it'll just mess with my stomach."

"We paid eighty-five dollars for this stuff. Skunked or not, I'm drinking it."

After that we wanted to go to the Arctic Circle. Mainland Iceland doesn't actually reach the Arctic Circle, but we figured we'd go to the closest place possible. The closest was the plateau of Melrakkasletta in the village of Raufarhofn. Along the way we saw a number of people riding bikes. They didn't really look like racers, and besides, we were in the middle of nowhere. I kept thinking, *Where the hell are these people going? I haven't seen a house in twenty miles. Man, these people are in shape.*

When we got to the area that was the closest to the Arctic Circle as we could get, it was a couple hundred yards away from where we parked. We couldn't get any closer, and we almost blew out the tires getting to where we were at that point. It was rocky, and there were birds' nests in the ground so we took the rocky pier. I had on my boots, and John had on his sneakers, which was a better move because they could contour to the rocks. When we did get to the shore, there was a little hut made out of sod. Many of the houses, especially the older houses, were made out of sod. We also found an old boat. It didn't seem like a lot of people went out to this area because it was so remote. On the way back, we took the shorter route, where the birds were nesting. They started to come out of their nests to protect them. It wasn't quite like the movie *The Birds*, with the birds coming after us, but it was bad enough that we ran back to the car. We had read that if you reach that point of Iceland where we'd been standing, that you can go to a specific organization and get a certificate that states you reached the Arctic Circle. We couldn't find the organization, though, so we left for our next stop.

We drove for a number of hours, and the waterfalls and scenery were still impressive. After a while we settled on an ocean-side lot by a lighthouse. We grabbed some bread and set up camp. It wasn't really a camp but a tent and my sleeping bag, as John was still staying in the trunk. Getting used to the twenty-four hours of sunlight hadn't set in yet—it never did. Most nights, no matter how much we drove or walked around that day, I couldn't sleep. That night we decided to go to a bar to see what the nightlife was like. There was only one guy there so we got a beer—ten dollars for one. After that, we knew why no one went out.

From there, we had pretty much exhausted what we could do or thought we could do. We decided to take a ferry to the nearby island of Vestmannaeyjar. The ride over was stormy and took a few hours, and by that time, we decided that we really couldn't afford anything, so we didn't eat. When we got to the island, we drove around and it was really spectacular, but we couldn't find a place to stay. We eventually found a campground in a defunct volcano. We both thought it would be a good idea to camp there. The grass was also high which made for a good cushion. That first night, I slept great and we decided to stay for as long as we could.

The next day I got up and went to the common area kitchen, which was a little more rustic than the other one. I really didn't care because it was raining and cold, and I just wanted to stay warm. John was still sleeping so I grabbed a few beers and talked to a few people from England. John had gotten a little more friendly with them than I had; they exchanged information.

After we got home, he tried to contact them because they arrived back in England on the day of the terrorist attack in London. He never heard from them, and we don't know what happened.

The other girl I talked to was from Quebec and had been traveling the world for over a year. She was making a fried spam and onion sandwich. She asked, "Do you want some?"

"No, thanks, I haven't been traveling as long as you, and I'm not sure it tastes all that good."

"You get used to this kind of food when you've been away for so long."

"I guess if I had been traveling for a year, I would be eating a lot of different things."

"Especially when the money is tight."

She was good-looking and friendly enough. I had met a number of people who had been traveling for an extended period of time and it seemed that they took on a far-off look. Kind of like they knew something you didn't, which they really did. This girl was abstract in her conversation with me, she talked about living in Israel for a few months and then moving on to New Zealand but she never really told me what she did while she was there. I'm sure my appearance had something to do with it. It was 7:30 a.m., it was a strange place, and I hadn't showered in a week. She was nice, though, and we continued to have brief conversations over the next four days.

That day it started to get very windy, and we were instructed by the attendant to bear down our tents. Luckily, we did have extra spikes and bound the tent so I wouldn't be blown away by whatever was coming our way. I felt safe enough and went to bed that night feeling reasonably confident. Because the sun didn't go down, I have no clue what time it was, but I heard a woman's voice call out, "You have to get out of the tent! You have to get out of the tent!"

At first I thought I was dreaming—until John came over and unzipped the tent.

"Fran, get out! There's a tornado coming!"

We both ran for the car. After an hour or so, I heard from the trunk, "You're snoring and the tornado is over, go back to the tent."

"Geez, John, you don't have to be a jerk."

About an hour later, the tent bowed in, and the top of the tent hit me in the face. Everything was shaking and the tent started to rip apart. I grabbed anything I could and ran to the car. After a minute, John climbed through the backseat, which I didn't know he could do, and unlocked the doors to let me in.

The next day, the tent was a wreck. There were holes everywhere, and we knew we had to fix it because we couldn't sleep remotely close to each other. So we bought duct tape and taped up the entire tent. One of the poles was also broken, and we tried to fix that. It broke again the next night, but I made do without it the rest of the trip.

That day we drove around the island and ended up on a dirt road again, looking for the lighthouse we had seen from the ferry. We found the lighthouse; it looked like it hadn't been used in years. The stairs to the top were rusty and didn't seem all that safe. It also smelled like dead animals.

As we were heading back to town, the air got really smoky, like there was a fire nearby. We couldn't find it, but we thought it was best to just get out of the area. On the way out, we took a different road and came across a huge wooden cross. It looked like it was about forty-feet high, and it looked a little creepy through the smoky air, but we took a picture anyway. Later that day, John went to the library to e-mail his mother, and I walked around the library looking at the Bjork books. There were rows of them. I never liked her singing, but I thought she was pretty good-looking; weird but good-looking. Then I walked around the town and asked a number of people in the stores about the big cross in the middle of nowhere. They all knew it was there, but no one knew why. I found out later that it was where the church used to stand until the volcanic eruption of February 1973 that wiped out the western side of the island.

That night, we just hung out by the golf course near the campground. We drove up a nearby hill, but turned around once we realized there were nails all over the ground. We figured it was to keep the local kids from partying up there. We also drove around and looked at the weather stations that dotted the main island. Most of them looked like they had to be accessed by boat, and the mountains were high. Then, whoever worked there, had to climb the wooden stairs to the top. They were steep and looked dangerous to climb, but I would've wanted to live there.

The following morning I decided to climb out of the volcano while John slept. I didn't know what time it was, so I grabbed a six-pack and started climbing. I got about a quarter of the way up, but it turned out to be a lot harder and steeper than it looked from the campsite, so I sat down for a while. I was a couple hundred yards up, and by that time I didn't feel like a beer and would have left them, except they were so expensive. John had gotten up, and it looked like he was talking to the British couple next to my tent and was about to take a picture. Later on, he told me that he was telling them that I don't like heights, but after the picture was developed, I saw that I looked like a dot on the side of a mountain. I should have kept going, but I had pretty much had it. It had taken me close to two hours to climb those couple hundred yards, so I climbed down to take a nap.

"Wuss, you were almost there."

I wasn't almost there. I wasn't even half-way up. I was close to the cave that was on my left but my desire to climb out of the volcano or even check out the cave had dissipated. I just said, "You didn't do it so shut up."

Later that day, we were talking to the British couple again, who told us, "We just went out and tried the puffins."

"How were they? I wanted to try them," I said.

"They were expensive and they are supposed to be a delicacy, and are only served at special restaurants. I liked them, but she didn't. She said the bird tasted like liver. I guess it's an acquired taste like snails or frogs legs. She thought they would taste like Cornish game hens."

After a couple more days, we left the island to get close to the airport, as we were leaving soon. It was stormy again on the ferry ride back, and there weren't many people aboard. The girl from Quebec, the one who had been traveling for a year, sat with me, and we watched the ocean without speaking. Then, on the loud speaker, the "Star Spangled Banner" started to play. We looked at each other, because it was weird to hear that song playing, but we found out the next day it had been the Fourth of July. Still, we were in Iceland, why would they play that?

When we got back to the mainland, we stayed in a couple of hostels, since we had to throw away the tent; it was just too beat up. The day we were leaving, we pretty much had most of the day to waste until our flight. We also had leftover beer and refused to waste it. We ended up driving around Reykjavik and hung out in a variety of isolated places. After changing into decent clothes in an abandoned rest area, we found a historic Viking boat and sod house. By that time, we had finished most of the beer and were having way too much fun and taking liberties that we should have been arrested for, but we hadn't seen a lot of police anywhere. John climbed into the boat, and I took some pictures. Then I climbed onto the roof of the sod house.

The flight back to Boston was a breeze for both of us, until we got to Logan Airport. Again, I figured I would have a problem with security, and I did, to an extent. I had changed my clothes in Iceland but I hadn't changed my underwear. I didn't anticipate what was going to happen—it had never happened before. When we got to security, they looked through my backpack and saw the pillow that I had stolen. Then they said, "Unbuckle your shorts so we can check the inseam."

I guess they thought I had something to hide and said, "My underwear isn't clean."

They laughed. "So what?"

After that trip, I bought dark underwear for my trips, but I never came across that issue again.

Chapter 13
Strange and Peru

The following school year was another great one. I had another group of strange kids—one kid was beaten up and broke his eye socket. The next day he sneezed in class and had to be taken to the hospital because his eye popped out a little bit. I never saw him again. Another kid didn't show up one day, and when I asked where he was, the students told me that he had been expelled for drugs the day before. Then he was arrested for beating the kid that turned him in. One of my advisees was arrested at the mall for stealing, and another was arrested for standing behind people at the ATM and stealing their PIN numbers. Another student stole some clothes from the mall and then tried to return them, hoping for the money. Instead, he was on the surveillance tape and was arrested. One kid stabbed another kid in the eye during fencing practice. I don't know why they didn't have their helmets on, but he was only suspended.

I wasn't fond of a local student named Lenny. He was in my World War II class and just a little strange. His mother was a doctor, and his father was a lawyer. He was rarely in school because his mother would call him in sick, and the school just kept him because he was a local kid. They thought if they didn't keep him, the father would sue the school. If the student was local and the student got in trouble, he was less likely to be expelled. This was because of the school's reputation as a reform school, and they were trying to get over that. There was one student who was expelled for bending all the forks in the cafeteria, but since he was from Maine, and nobody cared what people in Maine thought, he was gone. That wasn't bad for this kid. Most of the class he would be on the floor, crawling around under the desks and biting kids' legs. A number of times, kids had been arrested for stealing cars at the parking lot across the street from the school. Once a kid was arrested for stealing a car, but it was a stick shift, which he couldn't drive, so he stole another car, which turned out to be the security guard's car.

The first thing I didn't like about this kid Lenny was that he was a "close talker." He had no concept of personal space, and it was irritating. Then he plagiarized his own work on a previous paper. I realized this at home and e-mailed him the following day about it, telling him that it was illegal and that I was failing him on both papers. I told him that John Fogarty had been accused of plagiarizing his own sound after having been in Credence Clearwater Revival because of the similar sound of his new music. At assembly later that morning, Lenny came up to me and said, "I Googled John Fogarty, and he won that battle."

"All right then, I'll give them to the academic administrator, and he can decide."

"Okay, forget it. I'll take the grade."

"Oh, I guess that's because you just got caught stealing from the chemistry lab with material that looked like it could be used to make a bomb." He walked away.

What finally got the administrator's attention was when Lenny travelled with the choir to Germany. This kid dyed his hair blond and dressed in a Hitler Youth outfit. He was suspended for the rest of the year but allowed to graduate. He wasn't allowed to come to graduation, though. His excuse was that the pope had been in the Hitler Youth. I did find that odd that Pope Benedict had been in the Hitler Youth. I'm sure he was forced to be, but I really thought that would disqualify him for the position.

Besides those incidences, the school year went kind of normal—as normally as it could for this school. I was used to it but glad to be onto the summer. In 2006 we decided on Peru. It would, we hoped, be cheap, and we wouldn't get sick again. Once again, we went standby and left from Philly to Miami and on to Lima. We both had advisees from Peru. John's had been adopted by a family in Waterbury, Connecticut and the mother of my advisee had married a local man. I liked this kid, Kyle, and had his older brother, Paul, in class a couple years before. That year, Kyle decided to move back to Peru with his mother for school. He would e-mail me every once in a while, letting me know how it was going and telling me that he would return the following year and have to repeat his ninth grade year. He said that he would have to repeat because his Spanish was so poor that he had no idea what was going on in class.

By the end of that year, John and I had read what we thought were the necessary books on traveling to Peru. Later on, we read that some of these travel writers don't even go to the countries they write about—they get all their information off the Internet. I'm pretty sure it happened with the books we read for this trip. We seemed to be traveling blind but as usual would take our try at it. We had gone to the hospital to get our shots for the trip, since malaria and dysentery seemed to be prevalent, but as it turned out, we didn't get the shots because it took two weeks to set up an appointment, and we already had our tickets. The first flight John booked was to have a layover in Columbia, and it would have been cheaper, but we paid a little more to avoid the layover.

We got to the airport at about the same time as usual, 2:00 a.m. On the flight to Miami, I started to feel a little sick and when we got to Miami, I was really sick but I tried to hide it. It wasn't easy because I was pale and sweating a lot. John had his usual six to eight sodas, and he was tough to keep up with. In Miami, he took off for the bathroom and I sat on the floor, trying to get myself together. We finally got on the plane to Lima and John said, "You look sick. Are you going to be all right?"

"I'm not sure."

The Peruvian woman in the seat next to me seemed to be nervous because I was sweating so much.

In Lima, we had to wait for John's bags. By that point in traveling, I only brought the necessities, which always included toilet paper and had carry on luggage. I was hoping I'd get through customs in the shape I was in this time. I sat around waiting for John's things and thought about the Food Network show, *Traveling Sick*. I also tried to keep my head straight by singing songs to myself like The Band's "The Shape I'm In," and Eric Burdon and the Animals' "Got to Get Straight," but it wasn't working. John was watching the customs officials and trying to see who they were stopping. At the customs area, a green light would go on for people to just go through and a red one for people they were going to check. He finally said, "All right, let's go. They're stopping every sixth person in this line so we have to be together and get going to time it right."

I grabbed the cooler that we always travelled with (because most countries didn't have easy access to ice) and kept my head low. In most countries, the officials do want to check out your appearance but in South America they didn't seem to care.

After customs, we went to get our rental car. By that time it was close to midnight and most things were closed. Luckily, our car rental wasn't closed but they told us that we'd never rented a car.

"Yes, we did, here's the paperwork."

"Well, we don't have any right now, so you will have to take a taxi to your hotel. We will deliver it to you in the morning."

As we left, I whispered to John, "That's bullshit; they will not," but at the time we had no option.

Outside the terminal there were taxis everywhere and a lot of people, especially for the time. Our driver was helpful and said, "Do not go out at night, and put your luggage between your legs. A lot of times people will break the windows at stop lights and steal anything they see."

After close to an hour, we were at the hotel and John said, "I never would have found this place in the dark. Lima is a madhouse."

We signed in all our information for staying there, including our passport information, and went to the room. John wanted to get some beer, but I wasn't sure I could stomach it. He went anyway and got a twelve-pack. I took one sip and threw up.

He said, "Shit, Fran, you can't get sick in a third world country. You're going to be screwed."

"I'll be all right. You can drink all of them, since it's your birthday," and I went to bed.

Surprisingly enough, our rental car was there the next morning. We did the usual thing of writing any problems down that we could find with the car so we wouldn't be charged and then went for a ride. It was hectic, but other countries were worse. Again, there were a lot of manholes with no covers and people kind of drove and walked wherever they wanted. But we got used to it.

The first thing we wanted to do was get out of Lima, so we took the Pan American Highway south. We saw little shacks, no bigger than a regular-sized teacher's desk and not much taller. They were everywhere and that first day, we figured they were just markers where people planned on building their houses. Later on, we found out that these were their houses and that many times the women and kids slept outside while the husbands slept inside. Amazingly, for living in the small huts, the people were very clean; even their clothes were clean. We couldn't figure out how everything was so clean when they had no running water or amenities that we have. But each day, the dust was cleaned off the sidewalks, and everything was up to snuff. The other thing we saw a lot of was chicken coops; we figured that at least the chicken would be safe to eat. We drove for about six hours through some seedy-looking towns until we found a hotel with a closed garage. Most of the places didn't look too safe—we were concerned the car might get stolen.

That night we decided to take a walk around the small town. We went to check out the market. The food—chicken and other meat—was hanging on poles, and there were flies everywhere. It reminded me of National Geographic where locals were just used to the flies and almost didn't seem to notice, but for us, it drove us up the wall. I know that different countries and different nationalities have different ideas of cleanliness. I know that different nationalities adapt and have enzymes that can digest these foods, but we were both pretty sure we wouldn't be able to eat the local food. It looked like another beef jerky and Doritos trip. That was fine, but some of the people were gutting fish, and it smelled rancid. It was also crowded and the aisles were narrow, so we decided to leave.

The next day we continued to follow the Pan American Highway south. We were heading toward the Andes Mountains and had read about the police that we would probably have to bribe. We had agreed that we would act stupid in front of the police and say, "No habla." We figured, after reading the books, that we would have to pay about fifty dollars each time we would have to bribe the police. That day we drove for close to eight hours on our way to Nazca. In the middle of the Andes, there was a checkpoint and a toll. We hadn't seen anyone for a number of hours and thought we would get through to Nazca without a problem. The other checkpoints had been fine but at this one, two police officers stopped us. John said, "Hurry up and hide the camera. Here's my watch; put it somewhere so they don't see it. Take yours off too and hide it."

"My watch cost nine dollars from K-Mart. They won't want that."

"They don't know that, and mine was expensive. Hurry up."

The officer came over to us and started to ask questions. John got out the phrase book and tried to talk to him. It turned out that he wanted to confiscate our car because there were no reflectors on it. He stumbled through explaining that he didn't know that we needed them and that the agency didn't say anything about that when we rented it. The officer left to talk to the other officer, and we thought we were really in trouble. We were in the Andes and just about to be stranded. When the officer came back he had an amount written down for us to pay to keep the car. We forked it over and were allowed to leave. As we drove away, we looked in the mirrors and saw them laughing. John said that we probably paid them the equivalent of their monthly salary—it was close to $150. I had read that, at the time, the yearly average salary was about nine hundred dollars. We spent that in three weeks.

We continued to Nazca without any problems. We had read about the Nazca Lines that were supposedly made by aliens and were very big. They were of an alien, something resembling a plane, a shark, and other figures. As we got closer to Nazca, we saw a tower from which we could view the lines. We both were charged a couple of dollars and went up to see them but I never made it to the top. I wasn't impressed and really didn't care, but we didn't have a lot to do, and all of the Central and South American countries were starting to look the same. For the next couple of days we stayed in Nazca. It turned out to be a good time. We found a really cheap place the first night and went out to buy some beer. The beer was never refrigerated and finding ice was almost impossible. We had gotten used to the warm beer but luckily, we did stay at a place that night where the owner knew a guy who made his own ice. It took an hour and it only cost five dollars, but the block of ice was too big for the cooler. That hotel didn't have a TV and usually when they did, there weren't any English channels. I was glad that we at least had our own toilet.

That night we went up to the roof, and John took some pictures. Most of the buildings never seemed to be complete. It always looked like they were adding on to the buildings, but we never saw any work being done. Then we headed into town to buy T-shirts. I rarely bought shirts for myself because even the XXL shirts never fit. I always bought T-shirts for my goddaughter instead. Later that night, we tried to find some safe food to eat. That night it was french fries. At the restaurant, we looked at the two guys next to us, and they were eating a concoction that looked like soup with a corn cob and a chicken neck in it. Some other people were eating guinea pig, and I had wanted to try that, but the picture on the menu looked like a skinned puppy with its arms crossed, so I stuck to the fries.

As we left the restaurant, I thought we hadn't left a big enough tip for the waitress, so I ran back in and told John I'd meet him back at the hotel. After paying her some more money, she looked at me like I was an asshole. I realized as I walked back to the hotel that I probably insulted her, showing that I was a rich American. I really didn't mean to do that. We went to bed early that night because our room didn't have any lights.

We decided to find a little better but cheap hotel the next day. That hotel's bathroom had a window that didn't have curtains and looked up to the sidewalk. I could deal without a TV and lights, but I didn't like people watching me go to the bathroom. The next hotel was a lot nicer than what it cost. The room was great; it had lights and TV. While we were there we planned our airplane trip over the Nazca Lines. We booked our flight that would leave the next morning for forty-five dollars each and went out for food. That night we broke down and bought chicken and something that looked like a huge burrito. We ate the chicken, which turned out to be good and went to bed. In the middle of the night I got up and ate some of the burrito. About an hour later I threw up.

The next morning John got up and was about to start eating the burrito. I said, "Don't eat that, it's not what you think."

"Aw, what do you know?" as he took some bites.

"All right, but you'll be sorry in about an hour."

When we got to the airport that morning we had to fill out a form saying we wouldn't sue if we were injured in some way and John turned to me, "I don't feel so well."

"I told you not to eat it."

The planes were Cessna planes, and most of the people were couples. I didn't care about seeing the lines but the flight was fun. It took close to an hour and when we landed, John was worried that I might have thrown up. It turned out to be the highlight of the trip.

Later that day, we went to a small desert and hung out. We were stopped by the police again but didn't have to pay anything. They were just wondering why we were roaming around. From there, we moved on to another town. On the way to that town, we ran into a demonstration. We'd see two more after that, but this was the worst one. We got stuck in a traffic jam, and John got out to talk to the bus driver next to us. All of a sudden, all the people on the bus got off and wanted to climb into the car. There had to be close to twenty of them, and there was no way they'd all fit in. They apparently thought it would be safe to cross through the demonstration if they were with two Americans.

Right after that a big guy came up to the window and said to John, "I can get you past the burning tires and people if you follow my directions." He then climbed into the backseat. "Turn around and take a right on this dirt road. Follow that car."

It was someone's farm, and John was driving really fast, bottoming out a couple of times and scratching the side of the car on the branches beside the trail. From there we drove as fast as possible through a dried-out river bed. The river bed was about thirty yards wide and rocky, and at that point I was just hanging on. A few miles from there, the guy said we would be safe, and we both gave him a couple of dollars. We couldn't really understand what he was saying, but we thought he wanted us to drive him back. After he got out, I said, "Jesus Christ, what the hell was that?"

"That guy could have killed us anywhere along the way, and I wanted to scare the hell out of him."

During the next two demonstrations we just turned around.

We did see a lot of ancient Incan ruins, but they got boring after a while because they were all the same and seemed to be a tourist trap. We did want to see Machu Picchu. Why go to Peru without seeing that? When we got to Cuzco, which for some reason John kept calling couscous, we looked around for the cheapest deal to get to Machu Picchu. Every tourist agency wanted close to a hundred dollars each, so we figured it was a scam. The maps we had didn't show that you could make it up to the site yourself. We did finally find one that showed us that we could pretty much make it to the starting point by ourselves. We figured we'd do that.

We found the cheapest place we could to stay, and this time, we started to take advantage of the complimentary breakfast. It usually consisted of coffee, a biscuit, and orange juice. At least it would hold us over for awhile. That night it was cold, so we hung out in the room and read up on the altitude sickness that we possibly could get. Most of the books said to refrain from alcohol because that would be a hindrance. We knew that wasn't going to happen, so we also drank a lot of water.

The next day we tried to get to Machu Picchu, and we did make it all the way to the starting point. We had to go over a number of dirt or cobblestone roads, but we got there—and there were tons of people to travel with, if we were to go. I told John, "From what I've read, there could be up to three thousand people there at any given time. I don't really care to see any place with that many tourists."

"Me, either. Let's go. Tomorrow, why don't we go to Lake Titicaca and peer over the border of Bolivia since it is so close?"

We left early the next day and travelled up the Andes. We had read how many miles a person should travel up a mountain each day to get used to the altitude, but we really didn't think it was that big of a deal, and we didn't know we were going up as fast as we were. We watched the old women and men with their herds of sheep or llamas and kept going. At one point I said, "I'm starting to get a headache."

"You probably haven't been drinking enough water."

I drank more water, but the headache didn't go away.

As we got into town we didn't know where to stay or park, and we hadn't seen any police in a while. We definitely didn't see the officer in a raised tower, directing traffic, so we made what turned out to be an illegal right turn. The officer was irate, climbed out of the tower, and ran after us. We didn't know he was running after us, so we found a parking space in the town center, and John said, "I'm going to walk around and find a place to stay. You stay here and take care of the car." As we were talking about it, the officer came up to the window and started yelling at us. After we played our dumb routine, he realized we didn't know what we had done wrong, and at the time, we didn't. He then climbed into the back of the car, which made us both nervous, and tried to get us to pay a fine. He was in the back of the car for close to forty-five minutes. I just kept saying, "No habla." After the officer left, John told me he wanted us to pay three hundred dollars.

We found a place to stay. The parking lot was a couple of blocks down the road, and the wife was sleeping outside the hut while her husband was sleeping inside. It was about 2:00 p.m., and I thought it was strange, but once we opened the doors we both had our own problems to deal with. My face got really hot all of a sudden, and we were both out of breath right away. We hadn't been doing anything to be out of breath. We grabbed our things and helped each other with the cooler because we weren't sure what was happening, but it was happening fast. Both of us were in relatively decent shape, but what was happening? When we checked in, it was obvious to the attendant that things weren't going in our direction, so he grabbed our stuff and led us to our second-floor room. The second floor never seemed so far away. I'd read about this altitude sickness, but I never imagined it would be like this. Once we got in the room, I lay down on the bed and started hyperventilating. I had never had that happen to me before. John opened up the window and then he lay down.

For the next two days we just lay there, hyperventilating, throwing up, or going to the bathroom. It was the worst I have ever remembered feeling. Those nights we were pretty disoriented, so we left the TV on all night so we could make it to the bathroom. We didn't eat, drink, or sleep the entire time. On the third day, John felt well enough to go to the pharmacy and get altitude sickness pills. We should have been taking them before we climbed, which we figured out later. Over 14,000 feet in a day or so was dangerous. We sure as hell didn't drink while were there. We hung out another day for the pills to kick in and then took a half-hearted look at Late Titicaca. We did go over to the border as close as we could and looked at Bolivia. By then we just wanted to get down to a decent altitude.

By that time, it was close to three days before we had to leave, so we started to head back toward Lima. We were probably a couple hours south of Lima and sick of being in the car. We drove past one of the places that we had stayed before, when we had gone to the market and left because of the smell of the fish. This time it was blocked off because, we guessed, there would be another demonstration. John usually went in to get the rooms because I was pretty much looking ratty by that point. We found a cheap place, and he said, "You've got to see this room; it's got all kinds of things. Only one bed, though." When I walked in with the cooler, I guess the attendant put it together that we weren't a couple. We went to the room, cracked open some beers, and I flicked on the TV. Then John tried to go to the bathroom.

I said, "Wow, this place is a whorehouse. All there is on TV is porn."

"Right now, I don't care because there is no toilet paper in this bathroom."

I gave him mine, even though he always had ridiculed me for bringing my own toilet paper.

A few minutes later the attendant came up and said, "Sorry, guys, but this is the best room so you will have to leave."

"Can you give us another room? We'll pay by the hour. We're leaving the country soon and need a place to stay," John said.

"I guess so, but you only have twelve hours."

It was cheaper than most hotels so we agreed. The other room was really small and dirty, but I didn't mind. I got the bed and John took the comforter to sleep on the floor. We hung out for a while and bought french fries.

Lima was next, and once there, both of us were tired of the crazy drivers and demonstrations.

When in Lima John called the rental company after finding a room. They came over to pick up the car and didn't say anything about the scratches. The room turned out to be in another whorehouse, but I hadn't been sleeping anyway so the clicking of the high heels was bearable. We had two days left, so we walked around the town and oddly enough, there was a Chinatown section. We checked that out, along with the rest of town that we could get to by walking.

Downtown Lima wasn't the best place to go; it was really kind of glum. We had learned to find every public restroom that was available and use them as much as possible. The upscale hotels had clean, fresh restrooms and as long as it wasn't peak times, we could sneak in. We had done this crossing North America and in every country we had been to. They usually were stocked with toilet paper, and you wouldn't get sick from brushing your teeth in the sink—as long as you didn't brush for too long. John ran into that problem a lot more than I did. He drank the bottled water, but I didn't really trust it. He finally figured out that the bottled water wasn't necessarily cleaner. A lot of times the seal was broken, and it seemed that whoever was selling the water was filling it up with tap water, causing him to get the runs often. That day we did find a McDonald's. It had been a number of days since we'd had a decent meal, if you can call it that, but we were pretty hungry. We stayed there for close to an hour but we knew we couldn't gorge ourselves or we would get sick.

When I got back home, I got my mail from the post office. I always stopped my mail before I left for an extended period of time. The first piece of mail I opened was a warrant for my arrest. I was very concerned and called the Chester County Courthouse. The warrant was because I had missed jury duty sequestering. I told them that I was out of the country at the time and didn't know. I was told I would be contacted on the process. I was jury member 197 and had to call back after 5:00 p.m. for the next two days. Luckily, I wasn't selected. I hope I don't have a record.

Chapter 14
School and Panama

The following year was a little more difficult. Everything started to turn again; there had to be a new strategy to teaching with more computer work, and the computers never really worked properly. That's normal stuff, though, and happens everywhere, so complaining about it didn't solve anything. It was just something that needed to be done.

There was a new grading system and a new computer system that wasn't compatible with the system we had been using. There were all kinds of things but manageable things. The one major thing was the new AP teaching regulations. By that time, I had been teaching AP for five years and was somewhat happy with the outcome. I knew that my review depended on how the students did on the AP exam. I usually had five to eight students and two to three of them got fours or fives on the exam. It wasn't a great percentage but better than any other of the AP teachers, and some of them had doctorates. I also had been asked to go down to Texas to help grade the exam. I didn't go because it would've messed up my vacation. Then the College Board sent us information saying we all had to pass qualifications and register to be able to continue teaching our AP classes.

This happened during my sports requirement season, and I have to admit I milked it. I hated supervised play. Dealing with a bunch of kids who didn't want to participate in sports was a handful. I understood and, sadly enough, felt for them. It was unfair to them. Some kids don't like sports and are either messing around in the afternoon or studying. That was really true of the foreign students. Most of them slept less than four hours a night to complete their work. Not only did they not know the language very well but they wanted to excel. Most of the students didn't even have a choice of being there; they were forced to be there.

I continued to use this excuse about preparing the AP class with Jessy and Phil, saying it was a lot of hard work. It really wasn't all that hard, and it turned out to be easier than I thought, but I assured them they would be compensated for my lack of participation in it. I did work on this qualification thing, but I usually did that during my free periods and on the weekends. At the end of the season, I split the check for supervised play between Jessy and Phil.

After finally completing this ordeal that was about twenty pages, two months later I heard back from the College Board, saying that my syllabus wasn't accepted, and it had to be resubmitted. The first thing the College Board said was that there weren't enough letters in the submission name, since we had to submit it by our last names. I'd used my last name, but this time, I put FinnFinn and it was accepted.

I still didn't know what to do because I had been totally honest on my first submission. I did know that this was the first year the College Board were doing it so they might mess up in the process. If every AP teacher in the country had to create a syllabus, and there must have been thousands, they had to screw up. Supposedly, each submission was sent to a professor so that he or she could look over the syllabus and decide if it was college appropriate. They had to be inundated with this stuff and irritated they had to do it, so less information might be better. I had four templates to look at for advice on how to set it up. I really thought mine was better than their templates but too long, so I did what every teacher in the world shouldn't do: I supplemented my material. I copied most of the stuff and added some of the stuff that I had been using. To get turned down for this took two months; to get accepted for this took an hour and a half.

That was the biggest mess that year for me. I know other people had their own messes. People were getting fired or divorced, so my situation didn't seem like a big deal. That summer we decided to go to Panama. Panama seemed like a great place to go because I did use the information that I gathered in class, and the Panama Canal is a big deal. I had talked about how Teddy Roosevelt had gotten it started, supported the Panamanian rebels against Columbia; how he got Columbia to give Panama independence; and that more people died from the malaria and mosquitoes than from actually building the canal. I told them a lot of things and not since I had taught the eighth-grade American history class had I told them about the different ways to cross America and that the canal was the best option. Before that people either took the different trails (Cumberland, Oregon, etc.) across America, or the long boat ride down the Cape of Good Hope (which they were lucky to survive, due to the pirates and inclement weather). I had explained to them how people just settled where they ran out of resources. Most of these people were trying to get to the California Gold Rush, which pretty much didn't make anyone rich. Maybe Levi Strauss got rich, but that probably escalated later. The jeans were a good idea, though.

All this material I had read and studied but I hadn't seen, and I wanted to see it. Once we got from Miami to Panama, we found our hotel and continued on to the Panama Canal. It cost ten dollars to get in and, thank God, Panama was using U.S. currency—I was tired of figuring out the exchange rate for all the other currency. It was impressive although a surprisingly slow process for the ships.

Panama is a relatively small country, and we had close to three weeks there, so we took it slow. The first night we stayed in Panama City and again there were no manhole covers most of the time, and the traffic was nuts. The busses were all decorated and drove as they pleased, but the food was surprisingly good. Again, we did try to live off of chicken and beef jerky. Across from our first hotel, there was a stand where we bought chicken sandwiches and a few beers. For the most part, it was cheap. But crossing the street without getting hit was almost impossible, so the major cities had crossover walkways. Luckily, Panama City was the only major city we visited.

Trying to leave the city was tough, and we spent plenty of the trip kind of lost. We had done our research but really, there wasn't much to see. We spent most of the nights hanging out and talking to the locals. There were many Americans living there, because the cost of living is so cheap. We met one guy from the Bronx who had moved there with his wife. He didn't have many teeth, though he looked younger than me. We were right outside of the Darien, a dangerous area close to the Columbian border. We had read that a lot of people had been kidnapped there by drug lords and held for ransom. The guy said, "Yes, I have heard that people have been kidnapped. I've lived here for years, but I've never been there, even though it is only twenty miles away."

"Oh, we just got back, and it wasn't that bad," John said, even though we hadn't. We planned on going after we ate.

"You're braver than me." He picked up his chicken and left.

"John that guy is from the Bronx and barely has any teeth. We're from northwest Connecticut. The two areas don't compare. Maybe we should forget about it."

"No, we'll be fine."

After lunch, we headed to the Darien. The drive there was nice, and the scenery was great. The locals that lived in the area were few and far between. When we got to the area to cross into the Darien, there was a guardhouse and a bridge. No one was in the guardhouse so we just crossed over, trying to be cautious. On the other side of the bridge, the road turned to dirt and it became a thick forest. After about a hundred yards, we figured we had pressed our luck enough and turned around to head back to town.

The entire time we were in Panama, I never felt like I was in much danger. The closest we came to being in danger was when a man in Panama City was having a little road rage. We came upon it a little late but saw the outcome. I guess he had been rear-ended. We did see him get out of his car, grab some rocks, and start throwing them at the other car.

It's a beautiful place but there were American fugitives that asked us for money because they knew we were Americans. The first guy who asked us for food and money actually told us he was a fugitive from New York City. He was the first guy I met there. I had learned to ignore these people and keep walking. I always kept my wallet in my front pocket because these people have a tendency to bump into you and steal your wallet, and I had my passport in a pouch around my neck so it couldn't be stolen along with my identity. It sounds paranoid, but I know people this has happened to. I also always paid in cash and informed my credit card companies that I was leaving the country, just in case there was strange activity on my card. I haven't had a problem yet.

From there, we went to the city of David, then to a coastal town, to see if it was financially feasible to get a boat to one of the Bocas del Toro islands. The coastal town was a little seedy, and we tended to be followed around by people because they weren't use to Americans staying there. We found out later that most Americans—investors and real estate prospectors—went to the island, but they were rich and flew in or had their own boats. The hotel we stayed at was the only one we could find. It didn't have a sign, and if a kid on a bike yelling "Gringo!" at us hadn't led us to it, we never would have found it. It also had a barbed-wire fence behind which we could park the car for three dollars a night. The room was small, but for fifteen dollars, it would do, and the beds were surprisingly comfortable. The only problems I had with the room was that we were on the second floor, and the wooden floor moved a little as we walked on it; we could see the first floor through the wood. There also was the fact that the bathroom didn't have a door and the toilet wouldn't flush. Many times the power would go out. We finally asked a priest about it, and he told us that the power plants turn it off to divert the power to the major cities.

The next day we went to the pier and couldn't find anyone to ask about the boats, until an American woman docked with her boat. "How is the island?" we asked.

"It's very nice, and I only come over here to pick up groceries."

Right away, I didn't think we could afford it. This woman had her own boat, a nice one at that, and couldn't afford the food at the shops on the island.

"How expensive is it?"

"Pretty cheap, but you'd be better off leaving your car here. If you bring your car, it will cost fifty dollars, and you'll have to wait for the ferry. If you grab one of the taxi boats, it's only five dollars. You don't need a car anyway, since there is only one road."

So we got our stuff, told the hotel we would be back in a few days, and waited for the next boat. The boat sat six people, and the ride was thirty minutes. Other than the rain, I enjoyed the ride. On that trip I had only brought one change of clothes, so the first few hours were a little uncomfortable until I dried off. Once we docked, we bought some chicken burgers and walked around town, looking for a place to stay. The woman was right; it didn't cost that much. We found a room for thirty dollars a night. We knew it was a resort area—that was very apparent once we got there. There were more Americans than locals. We did ask one real estate agent, "How much would it cost to buy property here?"

"If you had done it five years ago, you could have gotten a decent sized piece of land for about five thousand dollars, but now it would cost you a couple million."

The next day we tried to hire a boat. "How much for a trip to one of the smaller islands?"

"Fifty dollars."

"That's way too much; we might be back," John said.

I said, "Fifty dollars to see a small island? I don't think so."

"Aw, don't worry about it; we'll find something cheaper."

Then a guy ran up to us and said, "I will take you to another island for ten dollars."

"I think we can swing that Fran."

He seemed to be a decent guy and took us to his house for breakfast—fried eggs, hash browns, and a beer. Both of us took notice of the sanitation while we were going to the island. The houses that were on stilts over the ocean emptied their toilets directly into the water. I love seafood but would pass again on this trip.

From there, he wanted to show us his property on another island that his family had left to him. "This property is now worth millions, and once I get enough money together I'm going to build a house here." He hugged his wife and child that he had brought along. It was a relaxing place, and I appreciated what he was doing, but I'm not a beach guy. "So where have you visited?"

"We just came from up north, and it was beautiful," John replied.

His wife shivered, shaking her head, and said, "We've never been there but we heard it's cold." At the time, she was wearing sweat clothes, and it was close to ninety degrees.

"No, it was in the mid-seventies."

The husband knew we were hot, so he grabbed some coconuts from the tree and smashed them against the tree to open them. I hate coconut; so does John. He said, "Thanks, but I'm allergic." I just said I wasn't thirsty.

After that we went back to our original island, and the man said, "You owe me forty dollars."

"What, that wasn't the deal? You said it was only ten dollars," I said.

"That was for the ride over to the first island. The second island is another forty."

"But we didn't even ask to go to the second island; you just brought us there."

"Forget it, John, let's get a beer." We walked away.

"You owe me money! You Americans are cheats!"

"Just keep moving, Fran."

The bars were expensive until we found a local place. The bartender said, "Most foreigners are too afraid to come into this bar."

"Why?"

"Because of the smell." It did smell like urine, but I was used to that by then. Most of the bars didn't really have toilets. If you were lucky, you got a trough, but usually it was a drain in the corner of the room with a hose for, I guess, other things. The first time I saw this I walked back out and said, "Didn't you just say this was the bathroom?" He said yes, so I just went back in.

After a couple of days I was getting a little ragged again, so I waited until John left and used his razor and other things that he had brought. He didn't seem to care that much. From there, we went back, picked up the car, and headed back to Panama City to catch our flight.

Chapter 15
New Administrator and the Dominican Republic

The following year there was a new administrator. The previous administrator was moving on and had falsified some documents for Middle States. I'm not sure how many but I do know that I was included as a member of at least one committee that I was never on. This new administrator hit me wrong right away. I've never been one to feel very comfortable in new situations, it takes time for me. At this school it took years but this new administrator just seemed way to comfortable right away. I guess the school was up for a big change. It seemed and many of the middle aged teachers talked about it, that every twenty or thirty years the school went through a metamorphosis. There always seemed to be a group of elder, then middle age, and then young teachers. There was never anyone in the middle of those groups to bridge the gap. Over the years, I knew I was under the microscope and was weary of what was going to happen to me. It wasn't going to be a pleasant end.

I became concerned when this administrator started to question my academic performance, but she wasn't following the advice she was giving me. She began to ask about my personal life; how I spent my free time, where did I go, etc. I made up some bullshit answers but I really didn't think it was any of this person's business. I didn't care about anyone else's personal life, but I've always been that way. I could care less what other people did.

This new administrator was beginning to ride me a bit. I think she was trying to get a rise out of me but that rarely works. It used to when I was a lot younger but not really any more. I did get ticked off but saved that for myself later or would vent to someone that really gave a shit, and they' re hard to come by. One problem that year started with a repeating student. That student e-mailed all the other students that he would sell all of his previous years notes for five dollars each, and if I changed the notes, he would return the money. Since this student was failing for the second time and wasn't very popular, most of the students forward the e-mail to me. I forwarded the e-mail to the administrator and received this e-mail back, "If you changed the information from year to year, this wouldn't happen."

I wasn't on good terms with this person so I didn't e-mail her back. I did tell the shop teacher and he said, "It's history; how do you change history?"

"I don't think she puts a lot of time into her e-mails or conversations. All the conversations I've had with her have been rushed or inconclusive. I feel like I'm intruding and interfering with something else she has to do."

Later on that year, the administrator started to call me into her office for every little detail. If I called in sick, she monitored my class the next day. If I went home for lunch or during a free period, she wanted to know why. Everybody did that. Most of us lived less than a mile away and in the same neighborhood. I'd even seen her on her way home in the middle of the day. But the major problem was that I didn't talk enough.

"My entire family is like that," I'd explain, "and I'm being penalized for my personality. I talk when I need to, not just for the hell of it."

"Well, you need to talk more."

There were a number of reasons that I liked teaching and a number of reasons I didn't like it. I liked the fact of being immature with the students but still having enough control that the students learned something. I almost could relate to them more and most of them understood when certain behavior was appropriate and when it wasn't. I didn't mind making up tests and quizzes. But the negative began to out way the positive. There was way too much of a power struggle among the teachers to gain favor from the administration. Also, many teachers didn't hold back on details, innuendos, rumors, etc. to get a head. It got to the point where an innuendo or rumor became fact. One incident could ruin your career.

I was tired of it and the only person's permission I needed to quit was my father's. I didn't want to disappoint him. I had already, by just becoming a teacher. According to him, the only true professions were doctors first and then lawyers second; a prep school teacher was close to the bottom.

The next day I went to school, and during sixth period I got an e-mail from the administrator asking to meet with me during my next free period. Right when I got the e-mail, I got really hot again, and a fellow teacher happened to walk in and read the e-mail. I said, "This is it, and I can't go through another day like I did yesterday. This half-ass job isn't worth it." I still had my ninth-grade class, which was about to come in, then a free period, and then my AP class. I started to compose an e-mail to the administrator, but I knew I had to keep my composure at least through this class. I knew what I planned on doing. I'd finish the e-mail, and they would never see me again. It was a tough class to get through and close to the end, another teacher came in—we shared the room. I finished my e-mail, which read: "Connie, so this is how it's going to end after seventeen years? In an e-mail? I'm not coming back for my AP class last period, and I'm not coming into work tonight. I feel like I'm being railroaded out of here."

It happened during my really good and cool ninth-grade class, which was better, in a way, because it made it a little easier, and if I had thought about it, I would have started to give things away. I would've given Kevin my stereo, because we shared music taste, and given whatever else to other kids. Once the bell rang I sent the e-mail and said, "That's it," and walked out.

On the way out, one of my advisees ran in and said, "Is it true?" I said good-bye and left, yanking off my tie. I've never been back and have only seen a few of the people that I worked with for so long.

About an hour later, the administrator called, leaving a message that said: "You're not fired, and I expect you back at school." I never answered the phone; I just sat there contemplating my next move.

Later on, a fellow teacher walked in. "What the fuck happened? I had to cover your last class."

"You were there; it's over, and I'm leaving to move west as soon as I get a cab for my truck. If I get it tomorrow, I'm gone, and they can deal with all this. Sell all my stuff or keep it; I don't care. I'm grabbing the important stuff, like my tax information and some clothes, but everything else is up for grabs, and I don't care about whatever money they owe me. Keep it."

"No, it's too soon. Think about it before just leaving. I've seen you do this before. The first thing you have to do is write an official letter of resignation, or you'll be fired and then you'll be in a bigger mess than you are right now."

"I can't write one. I'm not really sure how."

"Okay, I've done it a number of times. I'll write it for you." He went upstairs to my computer.

"You'll have to hand it in because I'm never going back," I said.

He handed it in the next day, and I got a letter from the headmaster, thanking me for my seventeen years of employment and wishing me good luck in my travels. Then I got a letter from the business office, giving me the information on what I had to do before I left and my pension information. If I wanted my summer pay, the house had to be impeccable or they would keep the $6,000. I didn't care, and if it hadn't taken two weeks to get my cab, I would have left everything.

The next morning Joe came over to see how I was doing before he went to school, and then Phil called to see how I was doing, but I didn't really hear from anybody else, which was fine because I wasn't all that close to any of them. Most of them were work friends at best, and I didn't expect much. I usually was only contacted when someone needed help moving because I owned a truck. A neighbor did say that people asked about me and would call him to see how I was doing. That day, I was told by the nice religious school that I had to move out the day before Easter. I also tried to contact the shop teacher who had been fired right before I resigned, but he never responded. I found out later that the school had put a gag order on him. He was told that if he talked to anyone about his situation, he would be kicked out of his house immediately. He has a wife and four daughters, and he couldn't afford that.

I still planned on just leaving, once I got my cab, but I was convinced not to be too rash because the economy was a mess, and my neighbor said that I could stay with him until I got myself together. I wasn't happy at all, but I did start to sleep better and my psoriasis started to get a little better. I spent my days cleaning the hell out of the house with my neighbor's help, after school. One day when I was upstairs, I heard, "You have a visitor."

Adam, a math teacher at the school, was there. By that point I had sold the majority of my furniture, and there was only one chair in the living room.

"I wanted to come over earlier," he said, "but Larry is my best friend, and I had to deal with him."

I had always liked Adam because he was real. He said it like it was, and he did his own fooling around on the side. He'd always been nice to me, and he had his own problems to deal with at the school. "Let's go to a bar. I know a good one in West Chester."

It was around 11:00 a.m., and I was somewhat surprised by his wanting to drink that early, and especially surprised by where he brought us. It was as close as it could be to being a strip joint without being a strip joint. There were three good-looking women, topless, dancing around the small club. I hadn't been to a strip club in years, and I never knew they opened up that early, but I was content with the situation.

We sat down and had a few beers with chips, and Adam kept on trying to give me dollars to put down the girl's underwear. Finally, I said to Adam, "I'm unemployed and going to be homeless in a week or two. Do you really think I'll put those dollars in their underwear or mine?"

We split the bill and left. It was fun, a little odd, but what I needed at the time.

After finally getting the house clean, it was time to move, but I wasn't sure if I wanted to move onto my neighbor's house. Fiscally, it would be the best move because I wouldn't have to pay rent, just split the bills. But I could afford my own place; it would be stupid but I could manage. My father had also offered me five thousand dollars to move out west, to move on with my life, but I didn't feel right about that. Months later, it seemed more likely I would take him up on it.

My neighbor and I have hung out for seventeen years but we are way different in almost every way. If we didn't like to travel, there would be nothing there to be friends. I know some people thought it was weird for guys our age to be friends and roommates, but I have way bigger problems to think about than what others think. He is very clean, and I'm not so much. He joked at first that we'd be like the *Odd Couple,* but I knew it was driving both of us nuts. At the time, I abided by the rules until things worked out in the paperwork of my life, but I didn't follow them to a T. The only example I'll give is that for some reason, the toilet seats had to be down at all times. I said, "We are two guys. Why?"

"Because my mother used to make us do it, so I just do. Also I put bleach in the toilets to keep them clean, and I don't want the dogs drinking it."

"I can understand that, but Bu can barely move and Kate has been real good since I urinated on her head when she was a puppy." Kate had stuck her head in the toilet to see what I was doing and I'm sure she got a bigger surprise than she expected.

When he wasn't around, I kept the seats up.

A few times it came down to my thinking, *Screw this! I'm grabbing my sleeping bag, pad, and Kate, and sleeping in the back of the truck.* I even looked into renting a trailer in a trailer park. Half of the time, I wanted to pump him full of beer so he'd go off on some kind of tangent and leave me alone. I just needed to figure things out. But I thought I'd ride this out and see what happened.

In the summer of 2008 I was in no mood to travel. I had no job, and I didn't want to spend any more money than I had to. My roommate was buying a lot of food that I didn't eat and I had to pay half.

John called to see where we were traveling to. He didn't know that I had quit yet. "If we travel, it better be to some place cheap, or I'm not going," I said.

"Why?"

"Because I quit my job."

"In this economy, what are you fucking crazy?"

"I had to, but you wouldn't understand." John and I never really shared too many feelings or any emotions. If either of us got close to sharing anything the other would say, "What, I'm I your therapist, shut the fuck up."

"All right. It's hurricane season in the Dominican Republic, so it has to be cheap."

"Okay, but I have to see if the kennel will accept Kate because it is a high time for travel. I asked Ginny before but she thought her dog and Kate would fight." It eventually cost me three hundred dollars for Kate to stay in the kennel.

We did our usual standby thing, but I was a little uneasy about what was happening with my life and started thinking differently. I was getting more ticked off about it as the time got closer. We had to leave for Philly at 2:00 a.m., so we went to bed early. I knew what I planned to do at the time, and got up at about 11:00 p.m. to drink a few beers. I didn't do it because I was afraid of flying; I like to fly. I did it because I hate the airport. All the lines and waiting made me crazy. If I had a few beers, I really didn't care anymore. I usually did that kind of thing, but this time was different. I started to say, "Screw it," and had too much. I decided not to go, and at 1:00 a.m., I went to bed again. John came into my room at about 1:30 a.m., mad because I wasn't up yet, and said, "Get your ass out of bed. We have twenty minutes before we leave." I was pretty disoriented at that point, which got him madder but I showered and left. A limo drove us to the airport again, and the driver was concerned that they wouldn't let me on the plane because I was kind of a mess.

I don't remember anything about the Philadelphia airport, but it was the best flight I had been on. It was during Hurricane Fey, and I pretty much slept the entire way. Everyone else was worried about the turbulence, but I slept fine. I was only awakened once by John because of my snoring. I had a great time on the way to Miami. In Miami, we had to hang out for a couple of hours, and we went our separate ways because John was ticked off about my behavior and I knew it was best just to stay away from him. My thoughts were a little different. I thought that I was almost doing him a favor. I shouldn't have drunk so much—that was a given—but I had no income and didn't want to be there.

The flight to Santo Domingo was fine, but the city was a wreck. By that time, we were used to the Central and South American thing—the streets and driving were crazy, and it took us four hours to find the hotel that we had booked. Within the first hour we saw a guy get out of his car with a pistol, like it was no big deal. After finding the hotel, both of us wanted to just hang. The attendant told us about the recent hurricanes and how the streets filled up with a couple feet of water; about the fish on the streets and the broken windows in the rooms. Our room had a broken window, and I made sure I got the bed farthest from the window, which wasn't by much. The window was cracked, but it looked like it was intentionally cracked, so it wouldn't shatter when the storm hit.

That night we had a couple of beers and left the city the next day. The Dominican Republic is pretty small so we took it slow again. What bothered me was the money. To my detriment, I never tried to get the grasp on the exchange rate in different countries. I thought it was costing a lot more than it actually was but it still wasn't as cheap as I thought it would be. After dropping Kate off at the kennel, I had stopped at one of the West Chester convenient stores to buy chew and told the woman I was going to the Dominican Republic because it had to be cheap. I was somewhat mistaken.

Food and beer were an issue again, because most of the people were very poor. I knew my stomach wouldn't take the spicy food, so I relied on pizza and beef jerky. Beer was tough because a lot of towns didn't have it, or we just didn't know where to get it. We did find one place and the attendant said, "You Americans drink too much." He's right, but we were on vacation and didn't care. What bothered me about the beer was that it was sold in forty-ounce bottles. That stuff gets warm, and in the Dominican Republic it was really hot. We were sweating the entire time. John's a walker and has walked the entire Appalachian Trail but in the Dominican Republic, he said, "Hell, no."

Everywhere was just hot and muggy. That first night, John said, "I can't believe the way you acted this morning."

"I didn't plan on coming because of my financial situation and was going to blow the trip off. I told you earlier this year that I couldn't afford it and didn't plan on vacationing. You said you needed to go and would pay for it. I knew that wouldn't happen and it was never brought up again. My father offered me money for a laptop so I could look for a job but I didn't want to take it."

"You should have; then you could have used that money for vacation."

"You have to be kidding? If I used that money for vacation instead of looking for a job he would castrate me."

We found most of the Dominican Republic to be resorts with their own airports. Most of the areas were off limits to people like us. We couldn't even get close to the ocean because the land by the ocean was bought up by resorts. We could only get by the ocean in Santo Domingo, and it wasn't all that nice. I'm sure it had to do with the hurricane season because it rained a lot, but there was no English-speaking television so we had no idea what was going on. We didn't know Hurricane Gustav was on its way. Good thing we weren't in Haiti.

The next day, while we were driving along one of the new resort roads, we saw a group of men working, and as we got closer, it looked like they were really ticked off about something. They had shovels and pitchforks, and it looked like they might be coming at us. There were no other cars or people around, and John said, "They're going to attack us." Then he sped up to get away from them.

As I looked through the back window, I said, "No, I think they're mad at each other. Wow, one guy hit the guy with the pitchfork in the head. He just crumbled to the ground. Let's get out of here."

Most of the time we spent inside because it was so hot, and usually, there was no air conditioning. It really sounds spoiled, but I was really hot and hadn't showered in five days. One day when it was raining, we stopped at a place for three dollars a night, but, even though I don't have a job; no, the place was gross. We asked people what was happening with the weather, and they just said, "Nothing; this is normal." Not for us. Shit, there were no routes or street signs, and we were lost most of the time.

Once we ended up at another hooker hotel. We didn't even know it was a hooker hotel because it was so nice. It was in a gated community, and each place was a bungalow. The owners were nice and seemed to understand our situation, so they let us stay for thirty dollars. It was the nicest place we stayed in. The air conditioner was the best, and it was clean and dark because there were no windows, but the only TV channel was a porn channel. It also had a swinging tray in the dinning room so if we ordered any food or beer, they didn't have to come to the door because the tray opened up to the outside. Man, this place was great, but we ate potato chips for dinner anyway.

John slept on the floor in the dining room, and I got the bed without any covers so he had something to sleep on. It was kind of a blessing in disguise for him, considering where we were. I hadn't slept in days and was finally cool enough to sleep. I'm not really sure what time it was, but John scared the hell out of me at sometime during the night. I woke up to him at the end of the bed, yelling, "Roll over, Fran! You're snoring!" I didn't sleep the rest of the night, and I started to get cold, which was strange, considering where I was.

The following day it started raining and didn't stop until after we left, so we farted around and went to what seemed to be a resort area. We didn't stop because it was too crowded, until some guy on a motorcycle pointed at the engine and yelled something in Spanish. We didn't know what he was saying but pulled off to check the engine, and it turned out we had punctured the oil filter and were leaking a lot of oil. We weren't sure if we would make it to a gas station. John had oil all over his hands, and we both thought we were in a bind. But we made it to a place to get it fixed. I thought we'd be paying a couple hundred dollars, and we'd have to spend a few days there getting it fixed. That meant we'd miss our flight, and it would cost more. We did find a very nice guy to help us fix the problem about an hour later, and he had a friend that dealt with this kind of problem. We couldn't believe it. It took less than an hour. The man climbed under the car, and that wasn't easy since it was a small car; he took out the oil pan and hammered the shit out of it. He then reinstalled it and put in two quarts of oil. We were done, and it cost thirty-five dollars.

The next day we had to get closer to Santo Domingo because we were leaving the next day. We didn't want to but the safest and closest place to stay was where we stayed the first night. It was more expensive than we liked but safe. It was raining like hell, and we didn't know why. Neither of us knew enough Spanish to understand anything when we asked. Santo Domingo was still a mess. The roads were flooded in about three feet of water, and the wind was going crazy. We knew something was wrong, and we had to leave as soon as possible. We saw cars stuck in the manholes that didn't have covers, and we were in a small car that was close to four inches off the road. I said, "John if we stop, we're going to stall, so keep on going."

"Let's ask someone why the weather is so bad."

"This is normal" was the reply again.

Luckily, this hotel had an English-speaking TV channel and that was when we found out about Hurricane Gustav. "Shit, Fran, we have to have a plan if this thing hits hard."

"I'm just going to crawl into the bathroom if the window shatters."

"I'm not sure that'll work because these things happen fast."

"Then what's your plan?"

"Ah, I don't really have one."

"Then why worry about it?"

I wasn't worried all that much about Gustav. What I was worried about was our flight being delayed, having to sleep in the airport, and that I wouldn't be able to get Kate for a few more days because of the holiday weekend. But we could leave the following day. When we got back, I started looking for a job right away. I was just kind of looking for something temporary and to waste some time during the day. I wasn't averse to heavy labor, so the first place I looked into was a delivery company.

I wanted to work the early shift because I didn't want to see anyone that I had possibly worked with. I was still a little uncomfortable with that. The early shift started at 3:30 a.m. or 4:00 a.m., depending on the day. I was up anyway, so that didn't bother me. I didn't have a laptop at the time, so I applied at the library and set up an interview. It went well, but I hadn't brought my birth certificate, and I couldn't get it from Connecticut in time, and I didn't know I could use my passport as identification. I also realized that the first person there got the job. The interview was at 4:00 a.m., and I was the second guy there.

After that, I went to another company and within an hour was hired. This shift started at 3:30 a.m. but it seemed that this company was more lax than the other company. I pretty much did the interview myself. I was given three training discs to watch, and the woman left. The only thing she asked me to do was pick up a box. I've been lifting since I was twelve, so I knew how to do that. I started the next day at 3:30 a.m. The disc said that the boxes would be only up to seventy pounds. That wasn't a big deal, but it was bull; some of the boxes were close to three hundred pounds and impossible to move alone. I ran into some of the same boxes day after day because no one was willing to move them off the truck.

During the interview, the disc said to report anyone doing anything illegal or making any condescending remarks. That first day, within close to an hour after starting, the guy I was unloading with broke into a box and started eating the candy. He asked, "Do you want some?" as he threw me a bag.

"No, thanks, I don't like candy." I threw it back. The place was so dark and the supervision so bad that no one would know any better.

Our supervisor was a little guy who spoke so fast that I never got his name. He would tell us what to do and then walk away. One day, I was working with a woman and nicked my hand, which started to bleed a little bit, and she said, "You have to leave and clean off your hand."

"It's no big deal. I've cut my hands plenty of times."

"Nobody wants blood on their boxes; they're afraid of AIDS."

"You can't get AIDS that way."

"Clean it off and get some gloves."

I got the feeling right away that I was working with plenty of messed-up people and that was fine, because I pretty much made my own bed. Some of these people seemed to be unstable. Maybe they were at the bar until 2:00 a.m. and went to work right after. A lot of times people were hanging out in the parking lot before work. I wasn't sure what they were doing, but once we went to work it was a free-for-all. They'd get ticked off if the boxes we were unloading didn't have the bar code up or to the right. Sometimes there was more than one bar code. One guy told me to ignore them and do it anyway I wanted. They didn't care if it read "Fragile" or "This Side Up." We just had to get it on the belt and get it to the next level. After a day or two, I decided to keep my mouth shut and take the eleven dollars an hour. I came to this decision after I told a fellow employee that I was thinking of moving to Montana, and he said, "I've never been out of the country before, and I'm not really sure where that is."

Every day I wanted to quit but I kept at it for a while. One day the supervisor came in and said, "Just collapse the boxes. Grab them from the top and pull all of them down."

"But some of these boxes say fragile or this end up."

"Don't worry about that, we'll take care of that later."

After that day I picked up my check and left. This time it was for good.

Most of the time when I was either teaching, traveling, or working for the distributor I was thinking about something else. I had been teaching for so long that it just got redundant, and I just had to look at my notes a few minutes before class. Traveling was a little different because we ran out of things to talk about. It almost got to a point where our conversations were, "You see that?" "Yup."

So I would think of songs because it kept me sane a number of times. If I didn't have music to fall back on, I would've driven myself crazy. I couldn't play a note of anything, except for the beginning of "The Sting," but I started thinking about music constantly when I was traveling. Since I woke up early every day, most of the shows were infomercials, so I ended up watching those and most of them were about music. I'd get a song in my head or I'd think about the first album I got or the first tape I got. I'd think about the best-looking women in bands. Or I would think of who the best guitarist was. Jimi Hendrix was great, and I used to tell the kids what he had in his head band, and what Sid Vicious used for gel, although he didn't know how to play. I always thought Eddie Van Halen, Eric Clapton, George Thorogood, Steve Miller, and Mark Knoppler were good. If I really got bored, I'd start to think of what really happened to Brian Jones—who really killed him? Why did Sid Barrett go crazy? Why did Bon Scott die in his car? What ever happened to The Band, and why was Ted Nugent in *Damn Yankees*? If I got desperate, I even thought about whatever happened to the oldest brother in *Happy Days*. He was there for a few episodes and then just gone. This would keep me occupied for a while.

After traveling so much, I needed to make some money, but I didn't want to go back to teaching, and it was obvious that this company hadn't worked out. I looked into a number of different areas, and my roommate gave me a time frame to get my things together. At first he said that we'd just move to Australia and get some crummy job there, but it got tense at times because we were so different. He said I had until February 1, 2009 to figure out what I was going to do, or I was out of the house. I looked into places to move and Ginny even said I could move in with her for a while, but that wouldn't work. I still get up around 2:00 a.m., and that would drive her family nuts. So I looked for a quick fix.

I started to look on the Internet for jobs and found some work-at-home jobs. I knew most of them were scams and that I'd probably get ripped off, but it was worth a try. One that I found seemed to be legit, so I gave it a try. I had enough money for this one but was told to watch out for pyramid schemes. I went for it anyway and signed up for another on-line company. They sent me the material, and it cost me close to $3,500. I was a sucker, and I knew it. When I started having problems, I would e-mail the people who said they were there to help me with what I should do and why no one was responding to my e-mails or calls. It was North American-wide, and I had to e-mail Jim in Michigan, Bob in Alberta, Canada, and Karen in California. I knew it was a messed-up situation but I followed through for a while. Eventually, Bob was out of the scene, and Jim stopped calling me back. Karen e-mailed me from time to time but wasn't very helpful. She just wanted me to follow through with the on-line training, but every time I got on it, they wanted more money, and I refused to do it. Finally, I e-mailed all of them about my concerns about the organization. I wanted to know about filing taxes and why no one was responding to my inquiries. I got an e-mail back, saying that, "We don't talk about negative things; we only talk about positive things." Taxes are negative, but they are a fact of life. I didn't want to be like Al Capone or Wesley Snipes; I wanted answers to how this company dealt with taxes. I figured after two weeks of no help, I would suck it up and call it quits. I even told them that I contacted lawyers about it. I didn't, but I'm sure that's why they haven't contacted me.

I also looked into a data-entry company, but it wanted my credit card number right away. I asked them where they were calling from. It sounded like India because of their accents and because I couldn't understand any of the people talking in the background. They said they needed forty-seven dollars, and I said again, "Where are you calling from?"

"It will cost you forty-seven dollars."

"No, I'd like to know where you're calling from?"

"I'll forward you to my supervisor." That person then forwarded me to another woman who at least sounded like English was her primary language. I asked her to send me the information on the company, which she never did.

A few days later I got a call again from the data-entry company and continued with asking them where they were from. The woman finally gave in and said, "New Jersey."

"Where in New Jersey? I pass through there all the time on my way to Connecticut."

I don't know a lot of towns in New Jersey and should have just mentioned towns in Connecticut, but evidently she knew fewer towns than I did. "Is it Hoboken, Elizabethtown, or Jersey City?"

"Jersey City." That was an obvious choice.

I knew she was lying and asked, "How far is Jersey City from New York City?" She couldn't answer. I didn't know either so she could have said anything.

After these attempts I decided to take another direction. What if I wrote? My father always told me I was a decent writer, especially after I wrote my mother's eulogy. I always thought writing was kind of a joke. No one makes money that way. The publishing company makes all the money; the writer makes squat. But it has to be better than making nothing at all. I took one creative writing class in college and had some stuff published, but I was only messing around. The professor was great. He had a doctorate but never wanted any of us to call him doctor because he said, "I'm not a real doctor, and if someone gets hurt they're going to expect me to do something. Saying I have a doctorate in English won't cut it. All I want you guys to do is write from your gut."

Why does every writer say that? "Write from your gut?" I've written from my gut and sent stories to my sister and a friend's wife, Cathy, who is also a friend. Both of them have said that my stories are strange. "To tell the truth, I just make up most of this stuff," I told them, which disturbed them even more. This story is true, but I have some others that have just been thoughts. Last night, I thought about a story about bagels. I wrote it down but really couldn't get six lines into it before I ran out of things to say.

In college, the papers were only a few pages, and I'd just write about things I did, like make fun of a girl that bleached her hair or what people think about while they're driving. I always thought of strange things when I was driving, like why the road signs are green. I learned later that the pigment in our eyes pick up green the best during dawn and dusk, which must stink for color blind people. I liked the class, but I was only making things up. The professor would blank out our names, and we would critique on each other's work.

Someone asked one day, "Who can write a three-page paper on stealing the springs out of his roommate's pens so when he gets to class, he couldn't write anything down?"

"Who super-glues everything in the classroom so not even the pencil sharpener works?"

"Who heats up the tongs in the cafeteria and then waits to see who is the first person to pick them up?"

"Who pours water on the seats so it looks like the person that sat in it wet his pants?"

"Who jams pennies in the door so the door won't open?"

"This person sounds like a jerk."

Sorry, that was me, and I enjoyed it.